ALSO BY BETTY ROLLIN

*First, You Cry*
*Last Wish*
*Am I Getting Paid for This?*

Here's the Bright Side

*Betty Rollin*

# Here's the Bright Side

*Of Failure, Fear,*
*Cancer, Divorce,*
*and Other Bum Raps*

RANDOM HOUSE ❦ NEW YORK

Published in the United States by Random House,
an imprint of The Random House Publishing Group,
a division of Random House, Inc., New York.

RANDOM HOUSE and colophon are registered trademarks
of Random House, Inc.

ISBN 978-1-4000-6565-3

Library of Congress Cataloging-in-Publication Data

Rollin, Betty.
    Here's the bright side: of failure, fear, cancer,
    divorce, and other bum raps / Betty Rollin.
        p. cm.
    ISBN 978-1-4000-6565-3
        1. Life change events.   2. Loss (Psychology)
    3. Life—Anecdotes.   4. Life—Humor.   I. Title.

BF637.L53R65 2007
155.9'3—dc22    2006049136

Printed in the United States of America on acid-free paper

www.atrandom.com

9 8 7 6 5 4 3 2 1

First Edition

Book design by Simon M. Sullivan

*For Ed*

# Contents

# Introduction

I woke up one morning and realized I was happy. This struck me as weird. Not that I didn't have all kinds of things to be happy about—love, work, good health, enough money, the usual happy-making stuff. The weird part is, when I thought about it, I realized that the source of my happiness was, of all things, cancer—that cancer had everything to do with how good the good parts of my life were.

When I thought about it more—and looked into it and started talking to other people—survivors, not only of cancer but of various other of life's infinite variety of bum raps—failure, divorce, illnesses and reversals of all kinds, death of a spouse, and so on—it turned out I was not alone. It turns out there is often—it seems *very* often—an astonishingly bright side within darkness. People more than survive bum raps: they often thrive on them; they wind up stronger, livelier, happier; they wake up to new insights and new people and do better with the people around them who are not new. In short, they often wind up ahead. There are even studies, scientific studies (!) that show that people often say they have benefited from the terrible things that have happened to them.

Coping well is part of this phenomenon, but there's more to it than that. Within each form of misery, there seems to be something of worth, a hidden prize waiting to be found. Sometimes it's found right away, sometimes not: a painful, debilitating divorce or widowhood can lead, gradually, to a new tranquillity within and without. (Not to mention the possible emergence of a swell new mate. Have you ever encountered the particularly dipsy-doodle joy of a newly married widow or widower? A person who thought love was forever buried with a deceased mate, but by golly, here it is again!)

Or if it's physical pain that has been endured, when the pain stops, you notice—and keep noticing—how well you feel. It's thrilling to feel well! But nobody is thrilled about feeling well who hasn't been feeling lousy, especially for a long while.

The prize—the bright side—may be as big as a barn or as small as a pea, but whatever its size, it seems to be directly born of suffering. When it's as big as a barn, it's an enduring gladness, and you may wind up feeling that whatever you went through was worth it (as I do). When the bright side is small, you may not feel that the bad part was worth it, but you come to feel that *something* good came from it, good that wouldn't otherwise have been there. Sometimes that means wisdom. Often it means the extremely good feeling that you get when you've been through something tough. It's a feeling of restored control and the sense of power that comes with restored control. Again, yes, coping figures into this; but mainly the bright side is what coping does for you, how it makes you feel about yourself and the world you live in.

The social scientists tell us now that as people cope successfully—and, they say, most do—they are uplifted, even elated. Having coped, you now know, as you didn't before, that you can Do It. You now know what you're made of. Having been through whatever it was that leveled you, you have come out the other side new and improved—as if you've had a sort of spiritual car wash.

The Harvard psychologist Daniel Gilbert, in his book *Stumbling on Happiness,* talks about people having a "psychological immune system that defends the mind against unhappiness in much the same way that the physical immune system defends the body against illness." And the worse the unhappiness is, he says, the more work the immune system has to do.

The bright side is almost always infused with gratitude. How many times have you seen on TV a family standing in a pile of rubble that used to be their house, weeping for

joy because they're alive? No family weeps for joy because they're alive as they stand in the middle of their
fully furnished living room.

Closer family relationships, a new appreciation of life,
a sunnier outlook on just about everything, a feeling, perhaps for the first time, of being entitled to put one's own
needs first—these turn out to be among the bright sides of
illness, according to a recent UCLA study of breast-
cancer survivors. Funny thing is, the study was originally
set up to examine the negative effects of the disease, but
the researchers were stopped short by women who kept
laying it on about the good stuff—about the bright side.

"More women reported improved self-image," the
study says, "feeling more self-assured, having survived
the adversities of cancer. . . . In terms of relationships
with other people, a high percentage felt more sympa-
thetic and compassionate towards others. About 80 percent felt that some good things had happened in their lives
as a result of the cancer."

The UCLA study was small, but it was followed by
larger studies with similar results. Some studies are so new
they haven't been written up yet. It's not that there's nothing negative in these studies; it's that, as the data rolled in,
"the positive was so prevalent, we could hardly believe it,"
says Dr. Patricia Ganz, one of the lead researchers at

UCLA. As a result, says Dr. Julia Rowland, director of the National Cancer Institute's Office of Cancer Survivorship, the field of research has shifted. And now benefits of other cancers are being studied, too.

Other researchers—again, to their surprise—have found similar results with other catastrophes, ranging from natural disasters to chronic illness. Susan Folkman at the University of California, San Francisco, found in her studies of AIDS patients that there was "a far more positive mood than negative." Youngsters who experienced Hurricane Floyd and the subsequent flooding emerged feeling better about their own competency than they had before. (At this writing, the results from Katrina aren't in yet.)

Not to be confused with the power of positive thinking or trying to see the bad event as not so bad, the bright side has to do with finding the good, whatever form it takes, within the bad and proceeding from there. And as they proceed from there, "people grow resources and gain skills, wisdom, strength they didn't know they had," Folkman says. "They review priorities; they have new meaningful goals; they live more in the moment." It irritates Folkman when the accusation of denial comes up. "This is not denial. These people know what's wrong. They just want to feel as good as they can."

We cheery survivors of bum raps meet with a lot of incredulity, but not from one another. We know what's up. What's up is better than anyone could have imagined. We ourselves couldn't have imagined it—before. It also turns out that if pain—physical and/or emotional pain—has been endured, one feels even more powerful and positive. "Paradoxical—or adversarial—growth" is what the studies call it. Meaning, the worse it's been, the better, stronger, more powerful one winds up feeling.

I do suspect that the ability to find the prize—the bright side—has at least partly to do with one's nature. And one's nature has partly to do with one's parents' natures. I think my own post-bum-rap cheer, for example, has a lot to do with my mother. My mother's glass was chronically half full. That kind of take on life is not the same as optimism, by the way. It isn't that my mother expected that things would turn out well. She thought they *had* turned out well. When I got breast cancer, for example, of course she was upset at first, but ultimately, she shrugged. What's a little cancer? Practically everyone has it. Besides, she added merrily, buying the surgeon's comforting cliché, "they got it all!"

But even if you don't start out with a positive nature, it's still mighty pleasant to have escaped from what might have been The End. The end of marriage equals the end of happiness; the end of a job means the end of self-esteem. Cancer means The End, period. Not!

People are so delighted and proud to be hanging in there. For some, it's a triumph just to be breathing. "I had X, but here I am," they exclaim—I exclaim!—as if they—I—had scaled a wall and made it down a rope to the ground. In a way they—we—have, and on the way down, moreover, we have learned a few things; we are enlightened, enriched, we have become improved versions of ourselves.

Here, then, are some of the things I and my fellow bum-rappers have learned. We've learned the hard way. Not, it turns out, a bad way to learn—especially about the bright side and how bright it can be.

# Here's the Bright Side

# *Power*

T o defeat despair can not only make you giddy, it can make you proud. It's the high of being in an athletic event of sorts and you've won. You feel more powerful than before. You *take* more power than before.

I am reminded of a career power story: a friend of my husband's, a mathematician, failed to get tenure at a college in New York. That's never good news. Failure to get tenure means not only that you didn't get what you wanted but that other people—people whose opinions matter to you—didn't think you were good enough. My husband's friend took it very hard. He stopped eating. He couldn't sleep. He could barely speak. Then he did some kind of mental backflip and decided to leave mathematics and enter law school. Today he is a brilliant and successful lawyer and, I think, no one has ever enjoyed being a brilliant and successful (did I forget to say rich?) lawyer more than this guy. His failure in mathematics laid the groundwork for his joy, his sense of renewed power over his life.

By the same token, many people could (and do) learn

about the bright side of divorce. When you are enduring the misery of a breakup, you cannot imagine that someone else is out there. (I know of some terrific first marriages, but now that I think about it, I know of more terrific second marriages.) Even less is it possible to imagine that *not* being married will suit you to a T—sitting on your own front porch at the end of the day, drink (and/or novel) in hand, with no one to hassle you about dinner. For some, that's loneliness; for others, it's freedom. Either way, the first-marriage misery, in retrospect, may seem like the best thing that has ever happened to you. Of course, it doesn't turn out that way for everyone, but it often does.

Sudden aloneness, even when sad—and I think it is almost always sad at first—can ultimately be empowering. I know a widow whose husband was in charge of all financial matters in their household. After he died, she had to take over. To her surprise, she became not only a financial whiz but a thrilled-with-herself financial whiz. There she was, doing something she had dreaded and feared, having fun! Making money! (Okay, sometimes not making money, but still it was fun.) The point is that as she mastered the money matters, the mastery felt good to her. A feeling of new power. This was one of those great marriages, and my friend has never gotten over her husband's death and probably never will. But here, at least, was a bright side. Only a side, a small side, but bright nevertheless.

A woman I know in Boston, now seventy-six, talks about her parents' divorce in 1945 as if it were last week. "It was more of a catastrophe than it might be today because divorce was so rare. There was such a stigma. Particularly because my father fell in love with another lady. It was just awful, not only losing a parent but seeing our mother so sad." Then she adds, "A year or two later, we emerged from the cloud, and I must say that I remember something very pleasant. We began to have such relaxed dinners. We'd talk about anything; my brothers and I had friends over; if the milk carton was on the table, it didn't matter. My father was so rigid. With him there, dinners had been so formal and tense. It was a wonderful change, really."

One of my favorite divorce-empowerment stories is about a woman who had a big job as a magazine editor (I'm changing some facts to hide her identity, as she wished me to). She had a marriage that she thought was fine, and two nice children, and a pretty house in the suburbs. When her husband became ill—some kind of heart disease—she quit her job to take care of him. He stayed ill for more than ten years, and still she remained at his side, as nurse, cook, housekeeper, and constant companion, not to mention single parent, in effect, to their children. When he got well, which he did rather suddenly, he upped and left her for another woman. Whom he married as soon as he and his caregiver wife were divorced.

How does one survive that kind of emotional assassination? Where's the bright side there? Nowhere in sight until a couple of years later, when the woman had a book published—a book she wrote as a way of dealing with her grief, going into debt in order to write it. It became a humongous bestseller, from which she achieved fame and fortune (not to mention great reviews!). Soon after, she remarried, and to hear her tell it, she's living happily ever after—with no bitterness, by the way, toward her first, rotten husband.

. . . . . . . . . . . .

How often does happiness—all the more exalted when it is unexpected—grow directly from misery? Answer: More often than one might think. What is the old saying? A blessing in disguise? Exactly.

Take failure. Failure can feel like a near death, especially if it's sudden—the sensation of dropping through a trapdoor without so much as a ledge to reach for. Ever been fired? It's like that. I've been through that one. So have a lot of people. I guess there are those who never recover, but my hunch is that most do and then some.

When I was twenty-eight, I was fired from a job as associate features editor (which meant writer) at *Vogue* magazine. It was my first serious job. I loved it, and I loved and respected, even worshipped, the woman who hired and fired me, which, of course, made the firing worse. She summoned me into her office one day and told me to sit down on the straight-backed chair on the other side of her desk. "I have to let you go, dear," she said, looking out from her round, red spectacles directly into my eyes. "You're a good writer, but you don't know anything." I have no memory of what I said—if anything—or how I managed to stand and walk out of her office. I remember only that I did not cry until I got home.

Maybe that wasn't the best turn in my professional life, but it came close. I wouldn't have left *Vogue* on my own, and it clearly wasn't the right place for me. I bounced around for a year or two and wound up at another magazine (*Look*), where I did not have to notice what the duchess wore to the opening of *La Traviata*. In the interim, I even managed to learn a few things.

And there was a sweet postscript: Ten years after I was booted out, *Vogue* ran a warm and laudatory review of my book *First, You Cry*—written by the editor who had fired me.

Annabelle Gurwitch is an actress who was hired by her

idol, Woody Allen, to be in a play of his. After her having obeyed an assistant's orders never to shake hands with or speak to Woody, "the accepted protocol when in his presence," she says, one day, during rehearsals, he spoke to *her:* "What you're doing is terrible, none of it good, all of it bad, don't ever do that again." She reports that she tried to soldier on, but when he later said, "You look retarded," it was hard. Not that it mattered, because she soon got a call from the director of the theater telling her that Woody needed to rethink the role (showbiz for you're history) and that Woody would write her a letter (which he never did). But Annabelle is a writer as well as an actress and knew instinctively that certain brick blows to the head might give you emotional concussions but that emotional concussions, to a writer, are Material. She promptly wrote a book about herself and other fellow sufferers called *Fired!* When I last saw her, she was on the *Today* show, successfully talking up her book.

A magazine editor friend, Katherine, was fired suddenly after fifteen years on the job, along with another editor who worked in a different department. ("Downsizing," the managing editor explained.) My friend and the other editor (a gay man) walked out of the building together in a kind of daze. They decided to have a drink. As they talked about what had happened, they both realized that, aside from the insult of being fired, they were mainly relieved. It turned out neither of them liked the magazine or the job or the managing editor or the editor in chief. What started out as a sobfest turned into a celebration. Two days later they took in an afternoon movie and subsequently had early-bird dinners together. They became best friends.

One day, they strolled into a bar they sometimes frequented, and the lady bartender—"a peppy little Brit," according to my friend—looked at them and said, "You know, I always like it when you two come in here because you always look so bloody happy!"

Steve Jobs, CEO of Apple Computer, gave a commencement address at Stanford a couple of years ago and told his favorite firing story about himself—how he started Apple in his parents' garage when he was twenty, built it into a $2 billion company with four thousand employees, how he hired a partner with whom, it turned out, he didn't get along and who, with the board's approval, fired him. "So," he said to the graduates, "at thirty I was out. And very publicly out. What had been the focus of my entire adult life was gone, and it was devastating."

What did he do? He started over. "I didn't see it then," he said, "but it turned out that getting fired from Apple was the best thing that could have ever happened to me.

The heaviness of being successful was replaced by the lightness of being a beginner again, less sure about everything. It freed me to enter one of the most creative periods of my life." During his exile from Apple, Jobs was far from idle. He bought another couple of companies, one of which, NeXT, was bought by (guess who) Apple, who promptly rehired Jobs, and as the world knows, he wound up back on top at Apple, newly powerful and, to hear him tell it, newly ecstatic.

Sally Fleming was twenty-eight years old when her house in Wilton, Connecticut, burned to the ground. Her husband was thirty; they had a three-day-old baby and a three-year-old child. No one was hurt in the fire, but they lost everything—things that were replaceable (except they were "way underinsured" and had no money to replace them) and things that were not, such as all of their family photographs plus Sally's parents' antiques, which they had stored in her attic.

"We hit rock bottom," Sally says. Then they did what people generally do if they can: they started over. And then some. Slowly, over a year, they rebuilt the house, meanwhile living in various rentals, including one they shared with a family of mice. The apartment had no furniture to speak of, little heat, and a ceiling that fell in. "All the while," says Sally, "I kept reminding myself that no one was hurt. And, as far as all the lost things were concerned, it gradually occurred to me that I was my own person and I didn't need the trappings. I just needed to keep my head up and I knew I was going to be fine and I was and it was a wonderful feeling. I wound up stronger than before."

Her parents were angry about losing their antiques, and for the first time, Sally says, she stood up to them. "It completely changed our relationship," she says, "for the better." Same with her husband. As she dealt with what had happened to them, Sally says, she developed a new sense of independence and confidence. "My husband wanted to leave Connecticut and go to Idaho and start a bed-and-breakfast. I said there was no way I was going to Idaho." They stayed in Connecticut. Sally decided to go to graduate school, which she hadn't thought she could handle before the fire, and got a master's degree from Columbia University in social work. "Learning to deal with what happened to us made me want to help other people deal with their problems," she says. "Really, the fire made me grow up."

. . . . . . . . . . . . .

An awful disease is a failure in the body. Or so it seems to the body's owner. This structure, which is you, which has always been there for you, has suddenly let you down. It's hard to trust your body after it does that. On the other hand: One can't help noticing how frequently one heals—how astonishingly the body asserts itself and makes itself whole again. I remember one small thing that impressed me about my own post-mastectomy healing. After surgery, even after several days, I couldn't raise my left arm, and it felt as if I would never be able to raise it again. I was given an exercise to do, namely stand near a wall and try to go up the wall, finger by finger, straightening out my arm as I went. It hurt, but after a couple of weeks, I could go all the way up the wall with an almost perfectly straight arm and no pain at all. I felt very strong doing this. Restored. Powerful.

At no time did I have physical pain; breast cancer doesn't really hurt and I never had chemotherapy. By rights, when it was all over, I had no claim for a medal. I gave myself one anyway. Other people gave me medals, too, in the form of looks on their faces of admiration, respect. All very good for the old self-image. Nothing like cancer to build self-esteem.

Patricia Spicer runs a breast-cancer support group on Long Island, New York. She tells of an elderly woman in her group who was worried about how her grandchildren would deal with her newly bald head, the result of chemotherapy. One evening the woman strutted into a meeting, pulled off her (hated) wig, and showed off her newly decorated head. With Magic Markers in hand, her grandchildren had drawn birds and flowers—plus a rainbow—from one ear to the other. She thought she would wash it all off afterward but decided, instead, to keep it, for purposes of showing it off, for at least a few days, until she had to wash her head—and then to have the children go at it all over again. Her plan, which she announced gleefully to the group at the next meeting, was to keep that up during the run of her treatments.

There is power, mountains of it, in humor. Cracking wise gets you through and pumps you up. After my first book, *First, You Cry,* was published, I got a lot of noticeably undepressing, often funny mail. One woman in Oregon wrote that she was doing fine until her dog ate her prosthesis. I laughed out loud and at the same time thought, Wow, this lady is a contender.

A woman from California wrote that after her second mastectomy her ten-year-old son tried to cheer her up: "Hey, Mom," he said, "now you don't have to wear the top of your swimming suit anymore and you can be a boy just like me!" (She added: "That was fifteen years ago. I'm okay. You're okay. Isn't life great?")

I remember assuring a group of patients in Ohio that

breasts aren't that useful. "You don't walk on them, shoot baskets with them, or hail taxis with them. I mean, what's the big deal?" That's a lie. It *is* a big deal. But not as big a deal as it was before I knew how to kid about it. In the joke there was power. For me, for them. I felt it then. I feel it now.

The truth is, illness is not a joke, nor is it an athletic event. You didn't "win" because of your skill as a goalie; you won because of your luck as an ordinary mortal who has, in addition, received good medical care. I hasten to make this point because I always wince when confronted with a battle analogy about cancer or any other disease. "He beat it; he (it's usually he, by the way) put up a good fight"; or, conversely, "He lost the battle." The implication is, if you're strong you win and if you're weak you lose.

Another implication is that you had a "fighting spirit." A good attitude, this implies, will help you pull through. A good attitude is always a good idea, but don't count on it to cure disease. No studies suggest that it does. I once interviewed Dr. Jimmie Holland, then head of psychiatry at Memorial Sloan-Kettering, the big cancer hospital in New York, on this subject. She's a great woman and a straight shooter, and she glared at me when I asked her about the attitude-as-cure concept. "Look, you can have the best at-

power

titude in the world and die, and you can be a complete quitter and live," she said. "That's just how it is."

A good attitude, however, can be useful—and not only for the person who's sick. A nurse once told me about a trick she used with whiny patients. She told them how well they were coping, how brave they were, how their families would be so proud of them; after repeated and major doses of that propaganda, she said, they'd start feeling proud of themselves and the whining would stop.

In that life had left me pretty well unscathed, for me cancer was, by far, the biggest blow to date. Although I knew my recovery had to do with luck and good medicine, still, I thought, Good for me!—not only inhaling and exhaling air but smiling! Laughing! Thumping my (breastless) chest about it! Making jokes! Yesterday a Jewish princess! Today a warrior!

So yes, you feel like a winner; never mind if it's a little inappropriate. I still feel that way, and it not only continues to cheer me up but continues to make me feel bigger-biceped than before. When you come through a bad spell, power marches in like a brass band. You're you again, but there's more of you than there was before. You fell down, but you got up. As you rise, you feel powerful. More powerful than you ever did before. And you are.

## Friends

To be sure, nobody spits in your eye when you've got cancer. But I don't know any sick person, widow, widower, tornado victim, or sufferer of any of life's grand assortment of punishments who is ever prepared for the avalanche of kindness, love, generosity, sympathy, pity (pity, especially at an early stage, is, I think, highly underrated) that comes from, it seems, everyone you have ever met in your life. People who are not even friends, whose names you might not even remember if you ran into them in the supermarket, people whom you may not even like, all are there for you. They show up; they call; they call again; they bring food; they bring presents; they ask for your guidance as to what more they can do for you.

Unless you are comatose, you are moved by all of this. You're probably moved to love these people back. Perhaps you've become better at loving back than you used to be.

I wasn't born yesterday. I know perfectly well that there is sometimes a component to all of the giving that is impure. (When is that not the case?) Sometimes you can smell it—the joy people feel in a world where awful things happen to others, that the awful thing has happened to you, not to them. They're actually grateful to you because, they reason—unconsciously, of course—if it *hadn't* happened to you, it might have happened to them. You have protected them from harm because it was your head that the brick hit when it fell, not theirs. Thank you! their hearts shout. Have another casserole!

My feeling about all of that, even when it was directed at me, was a big So What? When you're needy, you don't disparage the giver or the gift. And later on, when you figure out the human side to their impulse and realize, too, that the casserole had too much thyme, you are still grateful, as you should be. And maybe it occurs to you, as it didn't before, to send your own casserole—or store-bought cookies, whatever—when someone else is laid low.

I knew a law professor, Richard Uviller, a darling, gangly, six-foot-three leprechaun loved by all. After he died, five of his male friends got together, gathered the talks from his memorial service, which were wonderful, and put them into a small book with a photograph of Richard on the cover. They presented the book to his widow and his other friends: a gesture of such love and friendship that it made everyone, even people who didn't know Richard but had heard about or seen the book, feel good. His widow is not recovering speedily, but Richard's friends gave her a bright moment that I suspect will endure in its way.

The morning of my second mastectomy I woke up with a start. It must have been very early. Standing next to my bed was my friend Heidi Fiske. To this day, I don't know how she got in—they don't let people into hospitals at that hour—but there she stood, leaning over the bed rail, big smile. (Heidi has a gorgeous smile.) "Hi!" she said. "I brought you something." She held up a large container of coffee and a sugar doughnut, my favorite kind. Had I taken even a sip of coffee or a bite of the doughnut, the surgery would undoubtedly have had to be postponed. As everyone—except, apparently, my darling Heidi—knows, you do not dine for at least twelve hours before surgery, let alone twelve minutes. I explained this gently to Heidi. She looked disappointed but did a quick recovery. "Oh well," she said, "you can have it afterward!"

Will I ever forget the moment when Heidi Fiske appeared with an adorably inappropriate breakfast on a November morning that could not have been more bleak? Of course not. Would there ever have been such a moment if I hadn't been on the brink of cancer surgery? Of course not. Am I suggesting that surgery gives your friends an opportunity to do sweet things for you and, therefore, is a plus in life? Of course not. Just that it isn't a total minus, either.

That surgery caused me to miss another friend's wedding. On the second day in the hospital, as I was working through the dry chicken and limp string beans on my dinner tray, I heard a knock on the door. "Come in," I said, expecting the blood-pressure taker. But it wasn't the blood-pressure taker. It was my friend in full bridal regalia, including her bouquet, which she clutched with both hands while her new husband held aloft a small plate with a large piece of chocolate wedding cake. (I found out later that the sight of the two of them walking purposefully down the corridor caused a momentary dead halt of all activities on the eighth floor of Beth Israel's Silver Building.)

Two weeks later, I was home when yet another friend—a French woman, not one of my favorites, actually—showed up with lunch. (Notice how many people choose offerings of food. I loved this.) An exquisite lunch: smoked salmon, arugula salad with Gorgonzola cheese, pear tarte tatin, pink paper plates, and matching napkins were, one by one, retrieved from a large shopping bag and placed on the foot of my bed. "Voilà," she said. "We weel have a leetle peek-neek."

If not for cancer, I would not know how successfully one can freeze chocolate—a piece of information that I have found of lasting and inestimable value. My aristocratic German sister-in-law showed up one evening with a large box of Teuscher chocolates, the best. I wasn't in a chocolate-eating phase, and even if I had been and even if I'd offered a chocolate to everyone who came to see me, I knew I would still be facing the awful prospect of these gorgeous chocolates getting stale. I called the store on East Sixty-first Street and asked if the chocolates—many of them truffles—could be frozen. They said no. In desperation I froze a few of them anyway. The next day I took one of the little beauties out of the freezer. I waited fifteen minutes and popped it into my mouth. It was perfect.

I have not selfishly kept this knowledge to myself. I tell everyone who crosses my path. To be honest, my husband, who is generally uncritical of me, thinks I am quite boring about it. I guess Carol Channing thinks I'm boring about it, too. I interviewed her once in her dressing room and spotted a box of chocolates on her makeup table. Of course I told her the news, and instead of wild gratitude, which I thought I had every right to expect, I got a cold stare. Did I care? No. One day she—and others who have responded and continue to respond ungratefully—will get the message. I certainly hope so.

People who live in the country and in cities smaller than New York, where I live, bring homemade cakes and major meals. Sometimes they do this for days on end. Some recipients are too sick to eat, but when they feel like it, they know this cornucopia awaits them (and if it's chocolate, the cornucopia should be in the freezer, of course—all right, all right, enough).

. . . . . . . . . . . .

Not every friend is perfect. There are, for example, those who vanish. I still remember—and it is more than thirty years—going back to work at NBC News and walking down a corridor when I saw, coming toward me, a film editor I had worked with who was also a friend. He saw me from the distance—I know he did—and he turned and walked in the opposite direction, obviously to avoid me. What was he avoiding? I figured it out later when I ran into other instances of being avoided. There are people who simply don't know what to say to someone to whom something awful has happened. (I am forced to add that a lot of people in this category seem to be men.) I was not glad when faced with this behavior, but I was glad as I came to understand it, because understanding it is the only antidote to feeling hurt and angry, two feelings you do not need when you're sick or have been sick. Understanding this also comes in handy when you are the friend to the sick person, an experience that everyone over the age of twenty has surely had or will have.

Funny thing is that what you should do and say is such a duh. Here it is: Go up to the person—or call—and say, "How are you?" Then wait for an answer. If the person addressed doesn't want to talk about it, he or she can say "fine" and let it go at that. Or the person can say more. (In my experience, they *always* say more.) Either way, your friend will know that the question implies interest, caring. Which, of course, is the point, the only point. After that, do not ask a lot of nosy questions, especially medical questions. Let the person who's been ill run the interview. Doing so shows respect; your friend can say more or not; and an overload of questions is tiresome—and tiring—and can begin to seem intrusive.

Once, not that long ago, I remember taking the entirety of this particular lesson and trying it out on another NBC pal, whose wife had recently died, even though I kind of thought he, being male—a short, Italian, tough-guy type to boot—would probably not want to talk. Besides, we were in the newsroom, not an atmosphere conducive to the expression of grief, or feelings of any kind, except maybe tension. But it was obvious he didn't know or care where he was.

"You know what's hard, really hard," he said. "I have breakfast in the morning, and when I get up from the table, I leave the chair out. And when I come home at night, the chair is where I left it." Then his voice cracked, and he couldn't go on. I guess this doesn't sound like I did the poor guy a favor, but I think I sort of did. I think—I hope—that talking about the chair was better than keeping his story to himself.

. . . . . . . . . . . .

It's hard to call the following ex-friendship story a bright side, but there can be brightness in lessons learned, in clarity, even if the lessons are tough. My West Coast friend Noreen saw me through, among other darknesses, just about all of the crummy boyfriends I had until I got it right with Husband Two. A great and wise listener she was. A true friend when I first got sick, she called and called and called (before cell phones, when calls from California were expensive), she FedExed things for me to read, airmailed things for me to eat.

Then I got well. Not only well but astoundingly well. I had written *First, You Cry*, which, against all odds, was a success. Then it was turned into a TV movie that I actually liked, and I met my too-good-to-be-true-but-he-was-second husband. In the throes of planning our wedding, I was invited to Hawaii, where I had never been, to give a speech.

My husband-to-be was teaching and couldn't go along,

so I suggested to Noreen that she accompany me—she'd have to pay her airfare from Los Angeles to Hawaii but nothing more. I'd happily share my room, I told her. We arranged to be on the same flight from L.A. As soon as we disembarked, I sensed trouble, which at first, I ignored. My hosts met the flight and greeted me as if I were major royalty. I introduced Noreen, to whom they were as cordial as they would be to a lady-in-waiting. Noreen, I noticed, did not look happy.

By the time we stepped into the limousine, she was scowling. She had her jacket on over her shoulders, and by accident, I sat on her sleeve, which she yanked out from under me so hard I almost fell over. "Are you okay?" I asked. "Fine," she snapped. But she wasn't okay, and she got less and less okay. As soon as we entered the room, she pulled out a joint and began to smoke. I asked her not to. She gave me a look and continued. Things went, as they say, downhill from there. The next morning—the day of my speech—I told her I thought it would be best if we moved into separate rooms. She agreed, and that's the last time we saw each other or spoke.

I now know the name for the Noreens in one's life: foul-weather friends. Foul-weather friends, in case you've never had the pleasure, are nurturing with a vengeance when you're down, loaded for bear when you're up. It turned out she wasn't my only foul-weather friend, only the least subtle. The others—altogether only one or two—pretended they were happy for me, but there were signals that they were not. Signals like disappearance.

There's an in-between group: those who are true friends, but they're simply a bit truer when you're a mess. I accept this. I accept them. But I feel smarter about people and more grateful for friends of all stripes, overall a bright side of getting sick.

# *Doctors*

· · · · · · · · · · · · · · · · · · · · · · · · · · · · · · · · · · · · · · · · · · · · · · · · · · · · · · · · · ·

In a perfect world, doctors are both great at their work and nice people. In that sense, I had assumed the world was perfect, I learned otherwise, and it's a good thing. I now know, as I didn't before, that whether doctor or lawyer or dentist or plumber, the person working on your body or your lawsuit or your teeth or your kitchen sink should be professionally excellent, and if he or she is nice, too, that's okay, but nice is not the main event. Sounds obvious, but it wasn't to me. Where's the bright side in this? I'll tell you: getting smart. Or at least smarter. To me, smart is bright, especially when your life might be at stake.

When I first walked into my nice internist's office in 1974 with a small but palpable hard nut in my left breast, I was happy (what did I know?) to have him send me and my nut on our merry way. My instructions were to return in a year. About nine months later, however, when I was reporting for NBC News, I happened to be assigned a breast-cancer story. The story was about mammography and what a great diagnostic tool it was. Given that the nut in my breast was intact, the story made me nervous. So, feeling somewhat wimpy about it, I returned to my internist before the year was up. This time I had a mammogram, followed by a visit to a surgeon, followed by a modified radical mastectomy for breast cancer, described in the pathology report as "infiltrating duct carcinoma of left breast with marked desmoplasia of stroma." The size of the tumor— two centimeters by one—was considered far from small. In addition, the "surrounding breast tissue with focal intraductal carcinoma" indicated that all was not well within the duct of the breast. Ten lymph nodes, removed subsequently, indicated that my lymph nodes were all clear of cancer. Or that's what they thought at the time.

My internist, who I now knew might have caused my death by his genial instructions to ignore the lump for a year, is a lovely person. Number one, he is sweet and warm. Number two, he is a community-spirited kind of guy. Did—maybe still does—bicycle races in Central Park to raise money for awful diseases such as muscular dystrophy. A good person, no doubt about it. Still, he made a serious error in sending me away without a biopsy. It meant that my cancer sat there for nine months longer than it should have, time enough for it to metastasize. It just happened not to.

What was the lesson in this? Simple: When it comes to medicine, and all of those other things you pay people to do for you, nice (this is becoming my mantra) is not where it's at. Moreover, nice can be deceiving. Because my internist was such a sweetie, I trusted him—and his medical judgment. That trust could have been the death of me.

The converse is also true. I learned this from my mother's oncologist, who, I had reason to think, was a fine practitioner. Personally, however, he was a world-class jerk. Once I remember coming to see my mother in the hospital. She had lost her hair from chemotherapy by then, and she wore a little ruffled bed cap that made her look like Mother Hubbard. She had a bewildered look on her face. Apparently, her oncologist had just sped past, accompanied by his usual flotilla of residents and interns. She had wanted some information about the progression of her disease—she had ovarian cancer—but he wanted to talk about football. When she looked blank, he encouraged her to watch the game on TV. "It's on right now, Ida! Channel seven!" he told her cheerfully and then took off.

I suppose if she were near the beginning of her disease, instead of near the end, we might have switched to a doctor who more closely resembled a human being. But it was too late for that, and who knew if a human being would have been the technician this guy was. No guarantee of that, as I well knew.

Meanwhile, there were all of those nurses who rose to

the occasion. I admit to a pro-nurse bias. Anyone who has ever been in a hospital knows how much nurses matter, mostly because, unlike the doctors, they're there. And when you start to hurt, they're the ones with the magic needles. Of course, there are nurses and nurse's aides you want to strangle, but in my experience—and my mother's—nurses came through big-time. My mother's feelings about them were mutual. She forgot, sometimes, that they weren't her children. She worried about the ones who were single. (She didn't always like the sound of their boyfriends.) When she wasn't throwing up from chemotherapy, she gave them advice.

As for those doctors, everyone has at least one bad doctor story. How about the surgeon in Florida some years back who cut off the wrong foot? Studies of autopsies show that doctors misdiagnose fatal illnesses about 20 percent of the time. Then there was the guy (not that the lemons are all men, just the ones I know about) who knew quite well what was wrong with my arthritic, seventy-nine-year-old cousin but, while examining her, came up with the following words of comfort: "Look, you can't expect to live forever." Or the ophthalmological surgeon in Boston who felt obliged to inform my friend with eye cancer that "it almost always comes back."

Some hospitals now train medical students how to be

human, especially with patients who are terminally ill. I've seen these classes, and it seems to me the students fall into three categories: those who are already deeply and instinctively human and don't need lessons; those who do need lessons but are clearly educable; and those who should switch to careers in medical research involving rats.

In an internist one wants it all, kindness and competence both. That's because one's internist is there for the long haul. (At least you hope it will be long.) I've got one of those now. My research—several other doctors—told me he was well trained, experienced, a good diagnostician, et cetera. And during my first visit to him—an interview really, although I suppose he didn't know it—I could see he was not only "nice" but the kind of nice that I particularly care about. Which is to say I found him a straight shooter, patient, thoughtful, unphony, unfussy. He was even on time. Imagine.

It should be said that sometimes things go wrong with good doctors. Of course they do. Even good doctors occasionally make mistakes, and you just have to be careful that you're not the mistake. That takes both watchfulness and luck.

It is possible that the internist in 1974, who patted me on the head and sent me and my malignancy away for a year, was making a rare mistake. But after the entire episode was over, I did not even consider going back to him—even though I realized that my view of him as a bad doctor with a nice manner might not be fair.

During this process I learned something less than pleasing about myself. I learned that I am not forgiving. One summer, about five years after I stopped seeing this doctor, I was standing outside a theater in New York during the play's intermission. A woman came up to me, all smiles, and introduced herself as Mrs. Internist. (By now, *First, You Cry* had been published, and he had probably read it, including the less than admirable part about himself—unnamed, of course.) "My husband is right over there," she said, pointing in his direction. "I'm sure he'd love to say hello."

I saw him through the crowd, and I felt a certain rigidity come over me from head to toe. "Maybe another time," I said to his wife. She smiled again, much less broadly than before, nodded, and backed off.

That night in bed I replayed the scene in my mind. I should have gone over to him, I thought. He didn't mean it. He probably felt terrible about what happened, probably still does. Anyway, I'm fine, still alive, feeling well and all that. If I were in his shoes, wouldn't I want me to come over? Why were my feet glued to the pavement? After a few more tosses and turns, at around 1:00 A.M., I figured it out. He'd never apologized. If he had apologized, I think

I would have accepted that. But I knew perfectly well that a doctor can't apologize. Doctors can never apologize. To apologize is to admit wrong; to admit wrong is to risk getting sued. I should not blame them for not apologizing. But I don't blame myself, either, for not forgiving.

One needs to be tough-minded, I now know, about selecting any professional person whom you hire to make your bum rap, whatever it is, less bum. For a divorce lawyer, for example, you probably don't want your best friend's husband, who may be too nice a guy to get you what you deserve. Not that stinkers are necessarily the best professionals. But sometimes they are.

On the bright side, I have heard and read accounts of the loving relationships women—even some men—have with their professional rescuers, particularly physicians: oncologists, surgeons, internists, whoever it is who stands between them and disease like a bodyguard, blocking harm's way. Those relationships are intense and beautiful. Recently, I ran into an old friend, a burly, street-fighting politician who happens to have leukemia. We stopped to chat. I asked him about his health and, following that, whether he liked his doctor. He drew back and looked at me as if I were an idiot. "I *love* my doctor!" And then, in case I didn't get it, "I *love* him!"

I fell in love with my elderly, nearsighted surgeon

sometime between the surgery and his first postsurgical visit. He had rescued me, after all, from the awful thing that had entered my body. He was the first to see my scarred, flattened chest.

My surgeon was a very clean, ironed man. His doctor coat was white and crisp. His tie was knotted tightly. His hands were exquisitely bony and pale, the result, I imagined, of hundreds of thousands of thorough washings with foamy antiseptic soap. I loved him during the first mastectomy and during the removal of a malignant lymph node eight years later and during a second mastectomy a year after that—and will forever after.

Aside from feeling he was my protector from death, I loved him because he lied to me—I know this in retrospect. When he first saw me, he knew I had cancer, but he pretended he didn't know for sure. He knew I couldn't take more than a "maybe" at that point (I immediately sank to the floor in a Garboesque faint when I heard the "maybe"). A German Jew by descent, he was not given to emotional exhibition. No gusher he. Nevertheless, over the years of his care, I knew—or he made me feel—that he loved me, too. This exchange of love we had was, of course, not worth the bum rap that caused it. Still, I remember it, amid the terror, as a precious thing, a bright side. My eyes fill up just thinking about it, just thinking about him.

## *The Studies*

· · · · · · · · · · · · · · · · · · · · · · · · · · · · · · · · · · · · · · · · · · · · · · · · · · · ·

W ho knew? There is a body of research, an entire
field of psychology, that deals with the bright side of bum
raps. They don't call it "the bright side of bum raps." They
call it "post-traumatic growth," and what they mean is "positive psychological change experienced as a result of struggle
with highly challenging life circumstances." "A fundamen-
tal assumption of crisis," say the researchers, Richard G.
Tedeschi and Lawrence G. Calhoun, in their research-speak,
"is a potential for growth from negative life experiences."

The focus on post-traumatic growth, which took off in
the nineties, grew from studies of people coping with all
kinds of disasters, from hurricanes to the death of loved
ones. Like the social scientists studying breast cancer, researchers looking into these other traumatic events began
to notice not only that many people coped well but that, in
at least some important ways, coping well led people to
feel that they had benefited from the disaster. Even in bereavement groups, participants talked about perceived
benefits. Researchers took note.

The researchers explain that perceived growth tends to be reported in three general areas: changes in perceptions of self (survivors seeing themselves as having special status or strength, increased self-reliance, and heightened appreciation for life), changed relationships with others (increased emotional expressiveness, self-disclosure, and altruism), and a changed philosophy of life (reevaluation of priorities, appreciation for life). *Growth* means that people have "developed beyond their previous level of adaptation, psychological functioning, or life awareness."

A small point: *Benefit-finding* and *sense-making* after trauma are not the same thing. Both results are positive, but there is a difference between feeling that there was some benefit from going through the event and finding meaning from the event.

*Benefit* means the person has assigned positive value to the experience. Feeling, for example, that one appreciates life far more after it was nearly taken away. Christopher G. Davis, Susan Nolen-Hoeksema, and Judith Larson, writing in the *Journal of Personality and Social Psychology,* stress that, regarding benefit, "learning about one's strength in the face of adversity, or gaining insight into the meaning of life or the importance of relationships, may help to mitigate the feelings of loss or helplessness at the passing of a loved one. Such perceptions may preserve or restore the notion that one's own life has purpose, value, and worth; several theorists have suggested that these feelings are critical to self-esteem and well-being."

By contrast, sense-making does not necessarily imply benefit, except in the sense of feeling comforted from the belief that the trauma is "reasonable," even fair, that it is part of a nonrandom, orderly dispensation of events— God's will—even if those events are not benevolent. A smoker who gets lung cancer can at least continue to feel that the world is an orderly place, that there is a reason the bad thing has happened, and that the reason for his or her illness "makes sense."

## SOME SELECTIONS FROM THE STUDIES

> *115 refugees after the earthquakes of El Salvador in Janu-*
> *ary, 2001 were interviewed in the shelters about how they*
> *fared emotionally during their time at the refugee camps.*
> *Results show that most of the people affected by the earth-*
> *quake showed a consistent pattern of positive reactions*
> *and emotions. For example, 72 percent found meaning in*
> *the catastrophe; 88 percent used religious beliefs to cope;*
> *73 percent recalled some moment of happiness after the*
> *event; 67 percent reported positive learning; 64 percent*
> *reported that they had increased sense of self-efficacy;*

*30 percent reported growth in personal skills; 17 percent valued human relations to a greater extent. When asked whether they felt the experience would prepare them to face future disasters, the data were very similar: 64 percent said they felt more prepared to cope with a similar event in the future.*

. . . . . . . . . . . .

*1, 198 Vietnam veterans were interviewed regarding the psychological benefits and liabilities of traumatic exposure in the war zone: Psychological benefits, most notably solidarity with others, were found in those who experienced moderate amounts of combat. The findings suggest that feelings of self-improvement and solidarity moderated Post Traumatic Stress Disorder in those who had experienced moderate levels of combat.*

. . . . . . . . . . . .

*People with Rheumatoid arthritis were asked about benefits of their illness, 71.3 percent described interpersonal benefits. The most frequently described benefit was appreciation of support received from loved ones. Decreased pain, lower psychological distress, and the perception of fewer social constraints were related to these interper-*

*sonal benefits, as were lower levels of disability at a*
*12-month follow-up.*

. . . . . . . . . . . .

*At both 7 weeks and 8 years after a heart attack,*
*patients —345 men after seven weeks and 205 men after*
*eight years—were asked the following question: "Despite*
*all the problems and worries which your illness has in-*
*volved, do you see any possible benefits, gains or advan-*
*tages in this experience? If so, what are they?" Almost 60*
*percent of the men, after both 7 weeks and after 8 years,*
*reported benefits from the attack. In addition, those men*
*who construed gains from the initial attack not only were*
*less likely to suffer another heart attack, but fewer of them*
*had died when the same group was surveyed 8 years later.*
*A substantial number of patients said that the heart at-*
*tack caused them to reconsider their values, priorities,*
*and interpersonal relationships. The most frequently*
*noted benefit was that they learned the value of good*
*health behaviors (approximately 25 percent).*

. . . . . . . . . . . .

*After a tornado hit Madison, Florida, in 1988 (F-4 on the*
*severity scale with F-6 being the most severe) 42 people*

were interviewed; 39 of them again 3 years later. After the tornado, 62 percent reported increased closeness with others (52 percent 3 years later); 4–6 weeks after the tornado 41 percent reported that the community had become closer (24 percent 3 years later); 4–6 weeks after the tornado, 35 percent reported becoming nicer, stronger, more spiritual, and undergoing a change in life priorities (47 percent 3 years later).

. . . . . . . . . . . . .

In a study comparing how younger and older people feel about their lives, older subjects had significantly more positive things to say than did younger subjects. The elderly, who often have increased difficulty in their lives, such as deterioration and loss, often describe themselves as leading useful lives and feeling content. [More of same in the "Aging" chapter.]

. . . . . . . . . . . . .

Caregiving partners of men with AIDS focused on positive and meaningful events that helped them cope with the stresses of caregiving and bereavement. These included such occasions as ceremonies and social gatherings with close friends, which reinforced caregivers' beliefs and values regarding close relationships, and events in hospitals,

*where they were helping to care for their partner, which*
*reinforced their beliefs about self-worth. These . . .*
*processes . . . allowed these people to appreciate small*
*pleasures, interpret ambiguous situations favorably, and*
*find small victories.*

Research into post-traumatic growth is expanding. Current studies are focused on defining which areas of people's lives are changed most. Thus far, the five central areas identified are personal strength, changes in direction, relating to others, appreciation of life, and spiritual change.

Researchers are beginning to look internationally, to see if countries that are more secular than the United States also report the same types of post-traumatic growth. One question being asked is whether a kind of self-awareness of growth increases the likelihood of growth. (The researchers call this "growth reminding," summed up by a new awareness: "I am more vulnerable than I thought, but much stronger than I ever imagined.")

Make no mistake. As one reads between the lines of the studies, the suffering of the participants is apparent. But so, too, is their surprise—not unlike the surprise of the researchers—that their suffering, more often than not, has a stunning and unmistakably bright side.

## *Sisterhood*

For all I know, when I had my first mastectomy, in 1975, I was surrounded by other one-breasted women, but I didn't know them and they didn't know me. There was a reason for that. It's the same reason people with every other kind of cancer didn't know other people who had what they had. Secrecy ruled. Sometimes patients themselves were kept in the dark. Patients' relatives would ask doctors not to utter the C word, and often the doctors would agree. If the word was uttered, it was whispered, not spoken aloud. Cancer meant you were doomed. If it became known that you had it, you were thought to be a goner. Family would stand by you, but others, however guiltily, would often write you off. Some people thought you could catch cancer.

So if you had cancer—any kind—it was not only scary. It was lonely.

Not anymore.

In the mid-fifties a feisty breast-cancer patient, Terese Lasser, got mad at the secrecy that almost inevitably went with that disease—plus the lack of information that went with the secrecy—and started Reach to Recovery. Reach to Recovery was an organization of women (the first of its kind) who had breast cancer. Volunteers visited other women who had had mastectomies while they were still in the hospital, providing information and a gift box containing a "falsie," as it was called then, and "A Letter to Husbands," urging men not to shun their wives sexually. Volunteers were dedicated and energetic, but there weren't many of them.

By 1975 three famous women had spoken out about having had breast cancer, and their openness made all the difference to ordinary women like me. Shirley Temple Black, Betty Ford, and Happy Rockefeller made their decisions to come forward, and when they did, it was front-page news. (At this writing, by the way, all three are still alive.)

Still, one couldn't exactly call up one of these ladies and have a chat. And since no one else was talking, there were no chats to be had. I handled this by chatting, first, non-stop to my mother, who happened to be a world-class listener, afterward to anyone else who would listen (I think I must have cleared quite a few rooms in those days), and finally on paper, until I had a book. The hitch was that no publisher wanted to publish a book on such a grim subject, until finally a small house, Lippincott, which doesn't exist anymore, took a chance. And that was only because one of the editors there, Genevieve Young, took a fancy to the book and fought for it. Of course I was forbidden to use the word *cancer*—or the word *breast*—in the title, so I called it *First, You Cry*.

There was a small breakthrough in openness, not so much when my book was published but a few years later, when Mary Tyler Moore decided she wanted to do it as a television movie. Moore was, and is, an immensely beloved star, and I think when audiences saw her with half of her chest taped up (I always wondered if it hurt), they saw breast cancer as something awful, yes, but something awful that wouldn't necessarily kill you and something you could talk about and even continue to have a romantic life with.

At the same time, support groups had begun to form. It turned out I *was* surrounded by one-breasted women, who felt as lonely as I had. There were, in fact, a lot of them, and they all wanted to talk—mainly to one another. Today there are groups, hundreds of them, in every state in the nation.

I once helped organize a luncheon in New York to raise money for breast-cancer research. I'm a bit of a party giver and a partygoer, but this lunch was like no party I

have ever been to or given, before or since. We called it
"Celebrate Life," and we gathered together as many survivors as we could, including Bill Clinton's adorable
mother, Virginia (he was president at the time). The lunch
was held in a big, fancy room at the Plaza Hotel, and
everyone got gussied up—some in colorful turbans
wrapped around hairless heads—and there were speakers
and awards. Tears ran down smiling faces. Lower lips
quivered. And from noon until two, what might have been
an ordinary Thursday afternoon fund-raiser lunch at the
Plaza turned into an orgy of joy that was all about a bunch
of women who might have died, who were not only alive
but, at last, alive together. Here was a club of sorts that nobody in her right mind would want to join, but once in,
what a time we had! How tickled we were to have found
one another. How grateful.

Breast-cancer sisterhood is deep and wide; it's big
groups and small groups and a lot of one-on-one. How
many times have I—have we all—met a scared newcomer
and pulled her into the nearest ladies' room, lifted up our
blouses, and showed her our, however unusual, healed
chests. "See, it's not so bad. That redness will fade!" Or
offered a look at our reconstructions. "Look how soft it is!
Go ahead, stick your finger in it and you'll see!" Class,
race, age, status, all of that shoved aside, we became (I

don't care how sappy this sounds) sisters. Do you remember Marvella Bayh? She was the wife of the then senator from Indiana, whose son is a senator today. She was a tiny, refined, blond woman, and although we had just met, we found ourselves showing each other the scars on our chests as if they were new hairdos.

I've always been a girlfriend kind of girl, so all of this bonding with women who had been through what I'd been through came naturally to me. But there are more reserved and withdrawn women who bonded, too, and for them, I think, friendships were made that were closer than any they'd had before. Anyway, I've heard tell of this.

Need I say again that we'd gladly sacrifice the sisterhood to have been spared the disease? We're not crazy. But who expected such a bonus? I still have it. I'll be in a room, and a woman will find me and tell me she had breast cancer, and I'll look at her and nod, and she'll look at me, and we are close, even if it's just for a minute. I can't explain how nice that is. How important to me still.

Men have sisterhood, too. There are all kinds of support groups for men's diseases—prostate cancer, alone, has generated hundreds of groups. Us TOO and Man to Man are two of the biggest. Clarissa Potter, a social worker, who works mostly at Memorial Sloan-Kettering in New York, told me that they do better "hooking the men in" by calling

sisterhood

the groups "discussions" and "meetings" rather than support groups, but the men do come in and they do talk. "I've been extremely surprised at how emotional they are, how empathetic. They go deep fast," she says. "Fear helps, and so does facing mortality. There's a certain urgency to talk that wasn't there before." Men gather for support and comfort and advice and all of those other good things that can come from joining with others who have been through similar storms. The groups are too numerous to count, and they're not only about disease. (Most of the others are about divorce, single fatherhood, anger management, and abuse suffered in childhood.)

In or out of a group, once you let people in on your disease or disaster, one of the big surprises is that everyone you meet seems to have it, too, whatever the "it" is. And these days, it seems, they all want to talk about it! For some people (okay, men) sharing a bum rap is the only time they've gotten close to anyone outside their immediate families. I'd call that a bright side, wouldn't you?

# Born Again

Here's how it works in horticulture: Severe damage is (deliberately) inflicted on trees, shrubs, vines, and certain hedges in order to make them grow. Sometimes even roots are attacked! It's called rejuvenation pruning, and it can be the best way to stimulate or restore health and happiness to things that live in the ground. It takes time for the rejuvenation to happen, a year usually, but once reborn, the specimen will most often thrive.

There are unkind jokes about felons finding God, but often imprisonment—surely among the bummest of bum raps—does lead many into a spiritual awakening. Prison can shape people up in other ways, too. Some prisoners acquire an education they would not otherwise have had. And when they get out, they are likely to be at least a little bit smarter—and more employable—than they were before. Other personal earthquakes, too numerous to name, turn people upside down, and when they're right side up, they're different. Better.

I can't say I like Charles Colson, the Watergate criminal

who served seven months in prison in 1974 after pleading guilty to obstruction of justice. But Colson seems to have turned religious in a productive way and stuck to it. In 1976 he founded the Prison Fellowship Ministries, which helps prisoners and ex-prisoners and their families, and advocates for prison reform. It's pretty clear that, if not for his downfall, he would not have looked up. "Prison turned out to be one of the best things that ever happened to me," he says. "I never truly understood people until I was crushed. Until I lost everything and ended up in prison, I was never genuinely empathetic."

You don't have to be religious to be reborn. Joe Dawley is a painter who lives in New Jersey. He used to do garden-variety realistic paintings, from which he made a so-so living. Then he began falling, losing his balance, trembling inexplicably. It was Parkinson's disease. For Dawley, it meant the end of his career. His hands shook, so he couldn't hold a paintbrush still anymore. But in spite of his despair, he kept painting, just because he didn't know what else to do. And then a funny thing happened. Because his paintbrush shook as he painted, his paintings were now impressionistic. More to the point, they were good. Very good. A gallery owner saw them and gave him a show. Then another show. When I met him (NBC News assigned me to do a story on him), he and his wife were attending his one-man show in Palm Beach. Well-coiffed ladies and gentlemen in pink ties nodded approvingly at the canvases. Red stars began to appear on the frames, which meant the paintings were being sold. Joe Dawley is a small, mild-mannered man. I remember the expression on his face when I bent over to shake his shaky hand: delight, utter, stunned delight.

. . . . . . . . . . . . .

History—and fiction—is full of rebirth. Franklin Delano Roosevelt was a rich, patrician member of society, a distant cousin of Theodore Roosevelt. He had political ambitions but was seen as a bit of a lightweight, a dilettante, one who dipped into this and that, earning him the nickname "The Featherduster." Certainly he was not a man who had any interest in, feeling for, or understanding of the difficulties of ordinary people, which he developed, historians say, as the direct result of infantile paralysis. Polio struck Roosevelt when he was thirty-nine, and his new life, terrible at first, began. Ted Morgan, in his biography *FDR*, writes: "It was this spiritual battle, this passage from despair to hope, this refusal to accept defeat, this ability to learn from adversity, that transformed him from a shallow, untested, selfishly ambitious and sometimes unscrupulous young man into the mature figure we know as

FDR." This man, glamorous as all get-out, athletic and cocky and privileged in the extreme, had now to deal with being, in the language of the time, a cripple, a loser, washed up, pathetic.

The first sign of his new birth came in 1924, when, shackled by the steel braces he now wore and continued to wear for the rest of his life—they covered his legs from his feet to his hips—he managed get himself up to the podium at the Democratic National Convention to nominate Al Smith for president with the famous Happy Warrior speech. He was a changed man, triumphant. And, of course, that was only the beginning.

A psychiatrist I know who lives in Chicago is also an author, lecturer, wife, mother, social butterfly—on the record she has everything to live for. But according to her, she's been depressed much of her adult life and at times, off and on, has considered suicide. In 1995 she was sixty-two years old and on her way to yet another speaking engagement, this one in Boston. Shortly after the plane took off, she began to have horrible pains in her back. Because of her medical history, she knew what it was: a pulmonary embolism, and she knew it was serious. She says at first she was strangely calm: "I thought this could be the end, what I've been waiting for all these years." Still, she knew a megadose of aspirin could save her, and she found herself taking fistfuls. Later, she also found herself in an emergency room, wanting, after all, not to die. Which she didn't, but as a result of this incident, she says, her "inner life changed."

She went back to work, which was satisfying in a way, but she soon realized she didn't want to do it anymore—didn't want to see patients, didn't want to write books, didn't want to run around the country giving lectures. She begun to give herself permission to say no. Now that she had discovered how much she did not want to die, she decided there were a whole lot of other things she didn't want to do, either—and something else, entirely, she *did* want to do. She had, in fact, wanted to be a painter for a long time, but it hadn't seemed practical. After her transformation, she became a painter. She's seventy-three now and still painting. She says sometimes she misses "the action" of her former life, but on balance, this is the life she prefers now, a life—precious to her because she deliberately chose it—that she would not have had if not for her near death on the airplane.

At this writing there has been no "growth study" of the people in New Orleans who endured Hurricane Katrina. The suffering was so immense and intense that, no doubt, it continues for most of the victims. And yet . . .

The hospitals, along with practically everything else

that once stood in New Orleans, were hit hard. At Charity Hospital, six patients died before they could be evacuated. An unknown number died afterward. But many patients lived, thanks to the staff—the doctors, nurses, administrators, and others—who stayed on the sinking ship, working feverishly through days and nights to save as many lives as they could. One of the doctors was Ben deBoisblanc, who, several months after the disaster, informed *The Atlanta Journal-Constitution* that he most decidedly did not have post-traumatic stress disorder. "I have post-traumatic *elation* disorder! I've never felt more alive. I feel like it's awakened something inside of me." Before the flood, the doctor said, he was a "techno-geek" working in a technologically driven environment. Patients had become little more than diagnoses to him. "When we lost the technology," he said, "it was as though the patient emerged. The human being had been covered by this veil of technology, and as a result of Katrina, we peeled back the layers and all of a sudden we reconnected."

. . . . . . . . . . . .

As everyone knows, losing a mate is among the worst occurrences in life. I am old enough now to see friends becoming widows—and widowers—and I have seen their pain close-up. In most cases, over the months and years, sharp pain turns to dull pain. Still, pain remains. But not always.

My father died suddenly one evening after dinner in 1975, when he was seventy-two. My parents' neighbor tracked me down at a friend's house. When I got to their apartment, my father's body had already been taken away and my mother was sitting on the sofa in a kind of stupor.

My mother's reinvention of herself was so gradual that I don't think I grasped it until about two years had passed. She had been a loving and dutiful wife to a man who loved her but who had held her back in more than a few ways. My father had a brain—he picked up languages and musical instruments with ease and was good with numbers—but he had no sense of what people were about. Since people were my mother's specialty, that was a problem. She'd have an insight about someone they knew and he wouldn't get it and she'd get annoyed and then he'd get annoyed back. In addition, my father didn't like anything new. He wanted only to see his old friends, go to places he had been to before, talk about things he had talked about before.

As time passes, widows are often dropped by old friends. That didn't happen to my mother. My mother did the dropping. One day I noticed she had an entirely new pack of girlfriends, whom she'd met at the Ninety-second

Street Y in New York. She and her new friends joined a folk-dancing class; they studied poetry and Buddhism. Her new best friend, Rose, had been married to a Mexican painter who, years ago, was involved in a plot to assassinate Trotsky! My mother's other new best buddies were a gay couple who lived at the other end of her apartment floor. She joined a theatrical group at the Y, and one evening I found myself watching her in full costume and makeup playing (well, to be honest, overplaying) the role of the wicked stepmother in *Cinderella*.

She acquired a boyfriend. They had a weekly date, on Thursdays. Preparations for the Thursday evening date began early Thursday morning—outfit selected, hors d'oeuvres shopped for and prepared, hair and manicure done, apartment vacuumed, living room pillows plumped. I learned never to call her on Thursdays.

I don't think it's an exaggeration to say that my mother's personality underwent a transformation. She became girlish, occasionally giggly. She had always been a world-class worrier. She stopped worrying. My own mother, a born-again. I could hardly believe it.

Eugene O'Kelly is another born-again, different, though, from my mother and from Joe Dawley. Different from most people. He wrote about his rebirth in an astonishing book a while back called *Chasing Daylight*. O'Kelly was a big shot, chairman and CEO of one of the largest accounting firms in America, and by his own account he worked all the time. He missed virtually every school event of his young daughter's life. He traveled about 150,000 miles a year for ten years. During that period he had lunch maybe twice, he says, with his wife. When he was fifty-three, he got a diagnosis of inoperable brain cancer. His reaction (not immediate, of course): "I was blessed. I was told I had three months to live."

The "blessed" part, it turns out, was not that he was dying but, in his view, that he *knew* he was dying and so had a chance at a new, different life that only a death sentence would have brought about. (It helped that, somehow, he was pain-free.) He made a kind of happiness plan—there were charts and lists involved because that was how he did things. He stumbled at first—he was kind of a flop at "seizing the moment" as he desperately wanted to do—but he soon got the hang of it and, incredibly, had the energy to write about his transformation eloquently and convincingly. Shortly before he died—which he did, on schedule—he went out on a boat on Lake Tahoe. He described it as "the best day of my life."

I've seen other versions of this kind of awakening. That is, I've seen others soar at the end of life. I've seen hospice patients do it; I've seen it in Oregon. Oregon is the one state that allows terminally ill people to get a physician's help in dying when they want to. These people, perhaps because they feel in control of their destiny—and when their pain is being managed—have attained a kind of peace and tranquillity that is, in a way, enviable. Paradoxically, knowing they are in control of their death has allowed them to let go—and live.

Is there, then, a bright side of dying? There can be. To see it is to believe it.

# Men

Cancer improved my taste in men. Talk about bright sides; this, for me, was neon.

After Surgery One I got out of Marriage One, and before Marriage Two began, I drifted. That is, for a few years I was a single girl (I know, woman) in New York with one breast. I'll put it this way: You do not want to be a single girl *or* woman in New York with two breasts, let alone one. Having one made me feel entirely disadvantaged. In addition, I thought it was just me who looked that way. (Remember, all the others in those days were in hiding.) And besides all that, I no longer thought of myself as healthy. I felt fine, but I knew I had an untrustworthy body.

So who would have me now?

Surprise. Right out of the starting gate, I got a boyfriend. Then he dumped me (nothing to do with the missing breast), and I was out there again. In dark December no less. I volunteered to work on Christmas, and NBC obliged by sending me off to some wooded area in Pennsylvania where they reenact Washington's Crossing of the Delaware. God, it was cold. I couldn't believe those people who got themselves up in costumes (none of which involved fur coats) and chose to stomp around and seemed actually to be enjoying themselves. My producer was a lovely, funny guy, so that part of the thing was bearable, but it crossed my mind more than once that, later that evening, he'd be celebrating the holiday with his wife and I'd be home with my mother, with whom I had just moved in after my father died.

Work is great when you're miserable and lonely. I became a dynamo news correspondent that winter. Whenever something big and awful happened on the East Coast during the winter of '75–'76, I was on it. ("I'll go!" I'd shout to the bureau chief. "Send *me!*")

Along about March, people started fixing me up. (I guess these arrangements are called setups now, which always reminds me of bowling, but never mind.) I appreciated these efforts of friends, even though the results, as anyone who has ever been in a blind date phase can tell you, are depressing. If you thought before that there was no one out there for you, the parade of sad sacks (how could she or he think I could spend even one evening with this guy?) tells you you were right.

But I exaggerate. Now and then there was someone really nice. But then my sense of honor interfered. As each innocent candidate stepped into my living room, I felt obliged to inform him that he was facing someone who, unclothed, looked very weird. In time I learned to give the poor guy a drink first. Even so, understandably, I put some people off.

Gradually, though, I picked up on something I didn't expect: most men didn't seem to be put off, even if or when they saw the war zone on my chest. Maybe some of them were acting, but I don't think so. These were men who, after being informed about my affliction, gave me a look that said, So what? One time in particular, I remember carrying on about the awfulness of my torso (what a bore I must have been), and my date, a fellow writer, smiled patiently and said something I'll never forget: "You know, everyone thinks they look bad someplace."

Immediately, I remembered my thighs.

It was along in here, as my life progressed with the opposite sex, that I noticed something else. My girlish masochism had bit the dust. I had been one of those women drawn habitually to stinkers. Not abusers—no one ever hit me—but men who seemed to enjoy any opportunity to be mean. I found the meanness attractive somehow. No longer. Life had dealt me something nasty, and I lost my attraction to nastiness in human form. Not that I was clever enough to figure that out myself. A psychiatrist explained it to me, and as soon as he did, I thought, Yes, that's right. And I knew this was a good thing. Thank you, cancer.

And, most of all, I thank you for my second husband, Ed, who is just the kind of guy I might have found too nice, too kind before—too kind, especially, to me. We met at a party, and as we got to know each other, I was suspicious about the ensuing lack of pain. (Kind of like the song that goes, "This can't be love . . . ," but it was.) And in 1979 we got married and entered the stage of life called living happily ever after, the "after" of which has turned out to be far longer than I expected, twenty-seven years at this writing.

The same psychiatrist who explained this happy turn in my psychological life had an additional theory about why a man—nice or not—would be attracted to me. "You were—and are—a strong woman, but now your wings have been clipped; you're less formidable; more dependent perhaps. So men who are caring are drawn to you as you are to them." There's no science to back that one up, either, and any feminist would be appalled by such a theory, but it sounds right to me, so I pass it along.

The fact is, I underestimated men. I'm not alone in that. Over the years I've had letters from women with breast cancer who feared that their husbands or partners would no longer find them attractive and would leave them. In more than thirty years, I've never heard of that happening (any more than I've heard about women who walk out on men who have whatever. Still, women are not expected to be rotters, so they get no points for lingering). To be sure, the breast is part of one's sexual equipment, and its amputation is not alluring, but does a missing body part end love? I don't think so. On the contrary. Here I go again, basking in the bright side, but I'm reporting what I hear and see: the men I know about—and I've heard from some of them directly—actually seem to love their wives more post-illness.

In his smart and helpful book, *Breast Cancer Husband*, Marc Silver (he is one, himself) tells story after story of love and, yes, devotion. He describes the husband who, as he held his wife the first time after the mastectomy, said, "Our hearts almost touched." And he tells about the husbands who, like most, are not only loving but entirely there every step of the way. "We were always taking our pulse, so to speak," said one, "looking back on information we'd gathered, reviewing the information we'd gotten from doctors." Not that the loving husband necessarily does it right. There's an almost funny story about a husband who cries so much during visits to the doctor that, eventually, his wife asks him to do her a favor and stay home.

Of course, it's not only breast cancer that makes love bloom. A woman I know who lives in Stamford, Connecticut, had some awful nerve illness, and her Wall Street lawyer husband moved his practice to Connecticut just to be near her. After she told me this, her eyes filled up and she said something that struck me as odd at the time, but now I think it isn't. "You know," she said, "the sky is so—blue."

A man once wrote to me, "Somewhere in this land is a man looking for you. True, you have one less brest [sic] than most women, but when you come down to it, a man can only give attention to one at a time anyhow. It's the sum total of you that counts."

Another man sent me a pair of black lace bikini underpants (!) with a note that said, "I hope they're the right size. I know you'll be a knockout in them."

When breast cancer strikes, the biggest problem as far as mates and romance and sex go seems to be not in the woman's body but in her head. Shortly after my first mastectomy, I wrote about what was in my own head in *First, You Cry:* "I dreaded sex. . . . I did not worry that my husband would no longer find me attractive. He found me attractive. He wanted me. The crazy thing was, I did not want him. He still found me attractive, all right, but I did not. I no longer found me attractive. I was damaged goods now, and I knew it."

I got over it. And, as far as I know, most other women do, too. Like mourning any loss, it just takes a bit of time. And if you're lucky, time happens.

Sometimes it is the man who is hit, and the tables are turned. Say he is fired and suffers a loss of both income and sense of self because that job was not only something he had but something he was. I know someone like that—an engineering executive in California—and his wife came through big-time. What she didn't do was as important as what she did do: she wasn't pitying or funereal or critical or angry. She did strength and cheer. And she was good about letting him talk about it, which he wanted to do, especially at first. The relationship flourished—admittedly, it was pretty good to start with—and when he figured out another way to make some money, he relaxed about that part of it and found, of all things, that he was enjoying himself. Most of all, he discovered the joy of ordinary pleasures. "We're going to the movies tonight!" he said to me once on the phone, as if the movies were a trip to Tahiti.

So what's the point: that bad things can perk up a marriage, not to mention a life? With the operative word being *can*, I think the answer is yes.

# *Moments*

I have a friend who married a much older man. He wasn't at all well when they got married, but he was a darling and she loved him and she thought, What the hell? After a couple of years, he got worse—and worse still—and that meant a lot of back-and-forth to and from the hospital, sometimes by ambulance in the middle of the night.

As long as I've know them, they've been a supersuccessful, fast-track couple with a mad social life, which they both enjoyed and, to an amazing extent, continued to enjoy between double bypasses. Still, he began to spend more time at the hospital—and so did she.

My friend describes one evening after a particularly bad spell. Her husband had returned from the hospital that day and was sitting up in bed. She was still in her office clothes, but she kicked off her shoes, got into bed next to him, and clicked on the TV remote. They watched an old Humphrey Bogart movie, and as she described this scene, she said, "I don't think I've ever felt happier. It was the simple delight of being together, doing something dumb."

We're all headed somewhere. We have desires, goals, ambitions, yearnings. These are not bad things to have. They get us up in the morning. They propel us forward. They keep us energized, organized, employed, on track, sane, in a way. And yet so much of our lives is about what is going to happen, what we hope is going to happen, what we think *should* happen. And then trouble hits, sometimes big trouble, the kind that makes everything stop. If we emerge, there's a reward. Suddenly we are the beneficiaries of moments; small, delicious, giddy, sometimes tender moments that were probably available to us before but we didn't claim them or even notice them. Why not? Too busy, we say. But it's not busyness, really; it's a kind of stupidity. We think it's not important to look at the sky now. We can look at the sky tomorrow. Then, of course, we don't.

We're all like that—except, I suppose, Buddhists; they're the only folks I can think of who seem to have got the Moment thing down pat. As have the elderly. One of those aging studies—this one of emotional experience— showed that, as people age, "moments are savored, appreciated both for what they are and for their temporal fleetingness." The researcher Susan Folkman talks about people taking ordinary moments and "amplifying them."

The destruction, however incomplete, of the "should"s is what got me into the moment. When I emerged from my sick 1970s, I gave myself a present: Italian cooking classes. Since I was still working as a news correspondent, I knew I'd wind up missing some classes and probably shouldn't take this on, but *should* and *shouldn't* didn't hold as much sway for me as they had before. I could hardly wait for lasagna, which was due to come up the third week. Then something awful happened: I got an assignment to interview the First Lady, Rosalynn Carter. I liked Rosalynn Carter perfectly well, but she was no match for lasagna; not anymore. I bolted and took the lasagna class, and what made the day wonderful, I suppose, aside from the exquisite pleasure of learning to make lasagna, is that I had an astonishing lack of guilt about what I had done. (All the more remarkable because I told my boss that I had to miss the interview because I had a stomach flu and he believed me. I think.)

You can't groove in the moment if you've got guilt, but after you survive something terrible, guilt tends to loosen its grip. My presence at the lasagna class shows that the elimination of guilt does not breed virtue. But as far as virtue goes, I felt, in short: Been there, done that. Here's the big news: Lasagna is more fun.

All the more if you're dying. Could Eugene O'Kelly (the CEO in the "Born Again" chapter) have had such high spirits in a small boat on Lake Tahoe if he hadn't been near the end? Did he, for one single second, feel he should be somewhere else? Like at work? "The water looked like glass," he wrote in his book, *Chasing Daylight*. "There were hardly any other boats out, or it seemed that way. . . . We seemed to be riding not in the water but on it, skating along the surface. . . . I loved the sensation of being so close to the water. Or really, it wasn't so much that I loved anything, but just that I had the sensation, felt it fully." The Buddhists have nothing on him.

Once, my husband and I were driving along on a country road in western Massachusetts on our way to a restaurant. Our friends were in the backseat—she, a nervous backseat driver; he, the fairly recent recipient of a heart transplant, which saved his life. Construction on the road caused us to slow up. We were all feeling impatient—and hungry—except the transplant recipient, who kept shouting, "Look at that!" and a mile later, "Look!" again as he thrilled to the sight of the beautiful trees and flowers along the road. It was more than a year ago, but I remember noticing how enthusiastically he grabbed those visual moments on the road. I knew why: he had come close to not having moments, visual or any other kind, at all.

Seizing the moment often involves nature, but it needn't. I know a woman who lives in New York City. After her husband died, she spent a lot of time, she told me, "not moving, just sitting, sometimes reading, sometimes not." She had to go to work, so she left her apartment each morning and returned to it each night. But that was it. She turned down invitations. She sat.

Then, at some point, she got up and started to walk. She walked around the city. She walked on blocks she had never walked on before, and she saw things she had not seen before. It's New York, so a lot of what she saw were shops—Indian food shops in the East Twenties with their fragrant spices and condiments, usually sitting in barrels on the street; shops in the West Thirties where they sell nothing but buttons and spangles. For the first time, having lived in New York for thirty years, she took herself to the top of the Empire State Building. She was fascinated by the street musicians and their wacky instruments; by the short, muscular Hispanic guys expertly rolling racks of clothing in the Garment District. These walks, these moments on the streets of New York, started out, she says, as just moments. Then they became moments of pleasure. Small moments, to be sure, but bright nevertheless.

F.

Fear 1

## *Fear*

Y ou may wonder what fear has to do with the bright side. I am here to say there is a corner of fear that, if not bright in a merry way, is useful and often, I think, life-improving.

In its purest form, fear is the worst. It's right up there with pain. Like pain, fear seizes you and holds on. It takes you over. When you are in a state of fear, there's nothing else. Nothing. It's a whiteout. Usually, that kind of high-pitched fear has a short life span, but when you're in it, you don't know that.

Fear freezes you. But eventually you thaw. Because you have to. Life goes on. The fear is still there, but now, instead of being frozen in place, you're moving. You're moving, moreover, in a new way.

Bill Clinton, our brilliant and naughty ex-president, began moving in a new way after the trauma of his heart surgery a few years ago. Shortly after he came out of the hospital, he put what energy he had into fighting AIDS in a remote part of China, where AIDS was—and still is—

out of control. During a *60 Minutes* interview, Dan Rather remarked that the president seemed grayer and thinner. It was a different President Clinton from the one we knew, and he told Rather that he had just been to seven cities in China in eight days. "And I was truly exhausted," he said. "But I want to work hard. I don't know how much time I've got to live, and I want to make as much difference as I can." He soon went on, through his foundation, to fight the AIDS pandemic across Africa and the world.

Bill Clinton isn't the only guy whose fear tapped his altruism in a major way. A zillion people have followed that course. And it's probably not only to "make a difference." It's also to make a distraction from their own worries. I know a woman who could not stop thinking about her heart condition, even though she was diligently on her own case, doing all the right things to take care of herself. Finally, she did something very smart. She went to work two days a week as a volunteer for the Red Cross, and as a result, for at least two days a week, as she dealt with bloodied victims of car crashes, she thought a lot less about her ticker. Which, by the way, is still ticking.

Paradoxically, a thawed fear about death, however it comes about, makes people far more fearless about life. "I've always wanted to do such-and-such but was too scared" turns into "Wish me luck!" Somewhere, I suppose, there are those who are true to the cliché and "stop to smell the roses." I haven't seen too much of this. In the first place, we city people have never been into serious rose-smelling, and we're not likely to start now. Second, the survivors of bum raps I know have not stopped to smell anything. They haven't stopped! Maybe they stopped what they were doing before and started doing something else, but a general slowdown? No.

Survivors of disease, especially if it's been a close call, are big travelers. They move, they ski. They have babies, they start companies. They do good. They have *fun*. They do things they've been putting off. They put in the pool. They take Chinese (or Italian!) cooking lessons. They do the stuff they should have been doing, or might have been doing all along but thought, Sure, maybe someday.

Survivors make changes; some are positive, some negative. I myself perked up my life by getting not one but two divorces—one from a husband, another from another old friend. (In addition to the aforementioned Noreen.) We all have an old friend or two from whom we've grown apart. I found myself wanting a clean break from this person because, in truth, not only had we grown apart but we'd grown not to like each other much. Again, in the spirit of feeling short of time for a friendship that is not a real friendship, I thought, Enough. She made it easier by doing something mean to me. I was grateful. I wrote her a Dear Jane letter, and that was the end of it. We are both better off. There is pain involved in these life edits. Of course there is. But on the bright side, you realize how nice it is not to feel continuously irritated by someone who is supposed to be a friend. Plus, now you have more time for friends you like. Meanwhile, the friend you've divorced has more time for friends who like her. In the long run, I'd call it a win-win.

I still waste time. I sweat the small stuff. The dark side does not totally vanish. Fear isn't *that* good. It has not protected me from going to predictably stupid movies or getting fussed about a rotten meal in an expensive restaurant. But I go to fewer predictably stupid movies, and I get less fussed about both the food and the money. This mellowing, if that's what it is, seems to be permanent. (Of course, getting older helps.)

Sometimes women call me who don't have the results of their biopsies yet, so they're not even sure it's cancer, but the fear monster is at their throats. I can hear it in their voices. Some of them can't quite speak; they whisper. Their fear may continue after surgery, but not at that pitch. If there's no cancer, well, that's the end of it. (Except for those who are professional worriers.) But even if the news is bad, fear is displaced by the work of healing.

Healing takes energy and time and focus. It's demanding. Healing keeps you busy.

There isn't anyone over the age of thirty who has not had a dire fantasy or two on the way to a doctor's appointment. We are all at least a little bit afraid of being sick, especially if we are bringing along a lump, a bump, a cough, a pain in the wherever. We scold ourselves for being afraid. We know it's probably nothing. And usually, that's exactly what it turns out to be. But those of us whose lump, bump, cough, or pain has turned out to be not nothing have had our innocence destroyed. Our diagnostic virginity is no longer intact. We know, having had something once, that we might get it again. So we live with that knowledge. That is, we live with the knowledge that it could all be over sooner than we might have ordinarily expected it to be over. Not that recurrence means death—I know that from personal experience—but death is more likely to be an outcome of illness than of no illness. The question is, How do you live with this knowledge? What does it do to you? What does it do *for* you?

Mainly, I think, it wakes you up. You know a secret that a lot of people don't know (maybe they know it, but it's not real to them). The secret is that life does not go on forever. Somehow—I'm not sure why—knowing The End is a real possibility is not depressing. On the contrary. When

I absorbed The End as Reality, I found myself taking certain actions that were entirely delightful, such as leaving my first husband. I might easily have been one of those people who gets divorced after twenty years of marriage and thinks, Why didn't I do this before? Post-cancer I knew I had no time for shilly-shallying. I had given this sad marriage three years, and the moment had never been more right or ripe to say, So long, I don't have time for this. Which is to say, I don't have time for misery. How's that for a concept?

Okay, a while after my divorce I ran off with someone and it didn't work out, but never mind. I was now out of the marriage and ready for the rest of my life, ready for my second marriage, among other good moves, ready for Ed.

But a latent fear of The End did more than just spiff up my love life. It spiffed up my entire house, basement to attic. Professionally, for example, I liked being a news correspondent at NBC, but at heart I was a writer, and now, suddenly, it seemed obvious that I should write. What was I waiting for?

People do all kinds of terrific things when they wake up. A lot of them, like Bill Clinton and my friend in the Red Cross, help other people. Some of them never stop. They've been through something awful, and they know they have the power to take what they've learned and bestow it on others who are going through the same thing. We all do that a little bit, I suppose, but there are people who do it so continuously, with hearts so full, that you look at them and feel glad to be one of their species. Those people are the ones who will tell you they get more out of helping than the recipients do. Hospice workers say that all the time. They mean it, too.

In 1983 my mother was dying. In her opinion it was an unnecessarily drawn-out death, so she killed herself. My husband and I helped her. It was a good death. She died peacefully, gracefully, gratefully. I was stunned by what she did—that she actually did it. Very sick people frequently say they want to die, but often they don't mean it. Or if they do really want to, they're not about to make it happen. My mother, warm, steely, rational little person that she was, made it happen.

After any death of a person you love, you are numb at first, but when sensation returned, I knew I had to write about what she had done and about the difficulties we had had along the way. I also knew that, if I wrote about it, I could be letting myself and my husband in for a heap of trouble. It's illegal in New York, and was in all other states as well at the time, to help a person die. I checked with a criminal lawyer, who told me it might be okay because, technically speaking, my mother killed herself; in addition, whatever evidence there was of a crime would be evidence I'd be bringing against myself. Which, apparently, doesn't wash in a court of law. I listened carefully and picked up on the word *might* in "might be okay."

I decided to go ahead and write the book. I mention this here because I think it was that other fear that eased the way. This surprised me. First, I'm not brave. Second, until I thought about it, I hadn't realized I was still afraid of cancer. I remember thinking, What if it's not done with me? What if I have another recurrence and die soon? I'll be mad at myself for not writing this book.

It was easy after that. The book worked, and it got me involved in the physician-assisted-suicide movement. I had never been involved in a movement, and this is not the place to give a speech about how important it is for people like my mother to have a doctor's help to die. I will simply say that it has been one of the joys of my life to feel strongly about something and to act on those feelings. I had hardly ever done that before, except in my own selfish behalf.

Besides, the assisted-dying people are a great bunch. Board meetings are a blast. We've been going at it for about fifteen years now, trying to get physician-assisted suicide legal in states besides Oregon (where it is working wonderfully). I've gotten close to my fellow board members. I think it's not too strong to say we love one another.

The breast-cancer-movement people, most of whom have had breast cancer, are an equally fired-up group. There are thousands of activists, so they are not all buddies like our tiny death-with-dignity board, but they have the same glint in their eyes. Some of these women, before they felt their own residual breast-cancer fear and before they got involved in the breast-cancer fight, had no glint. Like me. Now we have a glint. Boy, do we.

. . . . . . . . . . . . . . . . . . . . . . . . . . . . . . . . . . . . . . . . . . . . . . . . . . . . . . .

There is an often overlooked bright side for every-one who is struck with a serious illness today as opposed to yesterday or, say, twenty-five or fifty years ago. If you had breast cancer fifty years ago, you wouldn't have been wor-ried about little things like your missing breast, because fifty years ago they would have taken half of your chest away in addition to the breast. Those surgeries were called radical mastectomies (as opposed to modified radical mastec-tomies), and they were awful—disfiguring in a way no re-construction could set right. Worse, years ago, if you were the unlucky victim of either breast cancer or any other kind, you might have died right away—or lingered for a while with inadequate pain medication. Pain medication is far from perfect today, but in the bad old days, it was as if you were *supposed* to suffer.

It's still pretty unpleasant to get heart disease, but com-pared with, say, twenty-five years ago, refinements in car-diac surgery have given years of life to patients who would previously have died. Thirty or forty years ago, they'd put a heart patient in a bed, give him some oxygen, and pray. Today, with a wealth of new medicine and technology available, they can do quick, life-saving procedures such as emergency angioplasty.

Treatments of infectious diseases, such as bacterial meningitis, are vastly improved. Years ago, if your appendix ruptured, you were as good as dead. Today, thanks to laparoscopic surgery and antibiotics, you are more than likely to live. Need a transplant? Years ago you probably couldn't get it, and even if you could, surgeons were far from having mastered how to make it work.

To name one cancer that used to be deadly and is no longer, testicular cancer is virtually curable today because of new platinum-based drugs. Drugs such as tamoxifen and Herceptin have saved the lives of thousands of women with breast cancer. New diagnostic techniques have caught all kinds of cancers early, lowering death rates. Chemotherapy is far more targeted than it used to be, making it more effective and less toxic.

Incredibly, the cause (or causes) of cancer is still unknown. One of the few exceptions is the proven link between cigarette smoking and lung cancer. But a lot of people get lung cancer who have never smoked. No one disputes that medical researchers still do not know all there is to know about cancer. That said, they know a lot more than they used to. So the point is, if you are diagnosed today, you have a far better shot at life than before.

And today, remember, if you get cancer, you have company. You have all those people who have it, too, and who are no longer in hiding. It is a disease that has become ordinary. That's bad, of course, but it's also good. It's not only that more people have cancer today; it's that many more people say they have it. They even joke about it. Believe me, fifty years ago there were no cancer jokes.

Fifty years ago there wasn't much in the way of prostheses, either. If you lost a breast, you'd probably wind up sticking your husband's sock in your bra. That was my own brilliant play in 1975. Aside from its lumpiness, a sock has no weight; so when you raise your arm, the sock rises, too, and can wind up somewhere in the vicinity of your neck. It's not a look.

Sometimes it annoys me that I am my husband's first wife, whereas he is my second husband. Yes, I feel that he appreciates me, but I know he would appreciate me more if he could compare me with the less-wonderful person he divorced. I make that comparison all the time, and he is the beneficiary. Which is to say he gets away with stuff because all I have to do is think back and he wins.

Reconstruction was my other second marriage, a total success—particularly when compared with the first, second, and third prostheses—the first being the sock; after the sock, a Dacron puff that also had no weight, and after that a rubber blob that had too much weight. The Blob was custom made by a Mr. Lee, who worked out of a basement laboratory at the University of Michigan. (In addition to breasts, he made other body parts—noses, ears, what have you, all lined up on his desk like trophies.)

I remember stripping to the waist and Mr. Lee covering me with a substance that looked like overcooked oatmeal. The "oatmeal," he had explained earlier, telling me far more than I wanted to know, was an alginate, which hardens into a rubber consistency. Before the substance hardened, Mr. Lee approached with a mixing bowl filled with what looked like creamier oatmeal. This was plaster. He then smeared the creamy oatmeal over the lumpy oatmeal and topped it off by wrapping me up in gauze. (It didn't end there, but I will spare you.)

A couple of weeks later, a pink blob came in the mail. Unlike the sock and the puff, it was good and weighty, but I knew right away that this would not be a lifetime solution. I wore it and tried to like it, but it was summer, and the backing, which was plastic, stuck to the flat place in my chest and made a disgusting sound when I pulled it off. I continued to wear the thing anyway, maybe because I had paid for it, maybe because I didn't want more surgery, maybe because I had heard that the reconstructive surgery they had begun doing (in the seventies) wasn't too great.

After a second mastectomy in 1984, I knew I couldn't face sporting two blobs. The combined weight of them would have had me down on all fours. But by then, great advances had been made in reconstruction—with more to come in the nineties. Never mind; what they were doing then suited me just fine. I had two choices: silicone or saline implants. I chose saline because, saline being water, I figured it couldn't hurt me if the implants sprang a leak. (Which they never have.)

So for me and for thousands of other women who have been similarly implanted: happy ending. I wound up with two small protrusions that, to this day, when I stick my finger in them, feel like mini–water beds. The best part of all is that the little winners stay up by themselves. No more bras! Not ever again! No man can possibly understand what it feels like to wear a bra every day of your life. It's a harness, and a woman is not a horse. One gets used to being bound in this way, but release from it is right up there with freedom from girdles and stockings.

I still have the Blob. I can't explain why I kept it. It's in the original box it came in from Michigan. Every once in a while I look at it. I can't explain why I do that, either. Sometimes it gives me a laugh when I imagine trying to sell it on eBay—or imagine a burglar ransacking my apartment, finding the box, opening it, and having a heart attack. Meanwhile, it remains in my closet, none the worse for lack of wear.

These days, there are all kinds of new reconstructive tricks, some of which are performed at the same time as the mastectomy, so there's none of that waking up to the sight of half your chest missing. And today, many women with breast cancer—if it's early-stage—don't even get mastectomies! Instead they get lumpectomies—just the malignant tumor is removed—because recent studies have shown that, for some early cancers, lumpectomies are just as effective.

You still won't feel lucky if you get a cancer diagnosis or have a heart attack. You're not lucky. But you're luckier than you would have been years ago. And in time you come to see it that way. I do. I think, Wow, a few years earlier and I would have a crater in my chest, not just a leveling. Of course, there is the other side: I also know, had I had the first breast cancer later still, I would've been put on tamoxifen or some other drug, being developed as I write, which might have prevented the second. But given that I'm still having birthdays, I consider myself more lucky than unlucky. By far.

# *Aging*

......................................................

I admit it's no fun to creak. And it seems to happen all of a sudden. One day you spring to your feet from a sitting position. The next day something amiss in your knee prevents you from springing and maybe even from rising. If/when you do rise, you forget about your knee, not because it feels all right but because your back feels worse.

Of course, that's the small stuff. Everyone knows about the big stuff that can go wrong as you age. But many of us who are old enough to have people offer us their seats in the bus (that happens all of a sudden, too) are dealing with only annoying knees and backs, and otherwise feel pretty good. If that is the case, aging can turn out to be, as young people say, awesome.

Let me count the ways: Number one, there's the extreme pleasure of being around. If you're old, you don't have to have survived a scary disease to notice that you're alive. Besides, even if you haven't been sick, surely some other rotten things have happened to you that now seem safely in the past. And if your memory is going, which it probably is, you've most likely forgotten at least some of those rotten things. And if you do remember them, you are likely to remember them in a kinder, gentler way. In a study where people were asked to recall positive and negative events from their past, older people had "higher levels of positive feelings" and fewer bad memories than younger adults did.

Aside from dealing well with their pasts, older people are champions of the here and now. In a large study (of four communities that included African Americans, European Americans, Chinese Americans, and American nuns, ranging in age from 19 to 101), a consistent pattern of age-based differences emerged. Compared with younger participants, older participants reported fewer "negative emotional experiences and greater emotional control." Older participants also reported less anger, sadness, and fear, and increased happiness(!). Aging was associated with "increased inner and outer control of happiness and sadness, as well as the inner control of fear and anger."

Another study (it's amazing how many of these come to the same conclusion) shows that older people are much more likely than younger people to sustain positive experiences and let go of negative ones. (This is where the "life's too short" notion comes into play. Not the mantra of an average twenty-year-old.)

Aging

Whereas in yet another study adults reported tensions with spouses, they reported fewer tensions than younger people have with children. In addition, they experienced less stress and were less likely to argue than younger adults. And among 32,029 Americans ages eighteen to eighty-nine who were interviewed by the National Opinion Research Center's General Social Survey, the sixty-eight- to seventy-seven-year-olds had the largest proportion—38 percent—of people who reported being "very happy." (Thirty-four percent of seventy-eight- to eighty-nine-year-olds reported they were "very happy," and the lowest proportion—28 percent—was among those eighteen to twenty-seven years old.)

I know of no study about grandparenthood, and not having had children, I bring no personal experience to this observation, but it would seem that being a grandparent is as pure a delight as adult people come by in their lifetimes and one of the biggest bonuses of being old. Better than having children, they say, for a bunch of reasons, including the one that's kind of a corny grandparents' joke: "The difference between my children and my grandchildren is that when I get tired of my grandchildren, I can say goodbye and go home." All fun and no work, they say—and, for the most part, no worries.

. . . . . . . . . . . . .

As you age, people die, and if you don't, that alone brightens the day. For me, opening the obituary page and not finding myself on it is cheering. Which doesn't hold when the people on the page are friends and family. Very elderly people suffer through these losses frequently, which considerably dulls the brightness of surviving. I know one ninety-one-year-old who ricochets between feeling lucky about himself and sorrowful about his vanishing friends. And of course there are those whose days, in general, are far from bright—people who are poor, alone, disappointed in what their lives have been, and forced to face the fact that the future looks both dim and short.

That said, so many of us are pinching ourselves because we're in a phase that we expected to be the pits and it's not. The negative expectation helps. Do you remember being a kid and thinking that, next to losing the softball game, being old would be the worst thing that could happen to a person? Now it seems to me the worst thing that could happen to a person is being a kid. All that confusion and pain; not having money or power; not having a car; not having a clue.

Whereas we are wise, or at least we feel wise, which is sort of the same thing. I think of wisdom as a level of comfort. You're comfortable with what you think and who you are, even though who you are may not be who you were supposed to be or wanted to be. And you're comfortable with what you know and what you don't—and may never—know. This adds up to a nice kind of letting go, which I think accounts for the mellowness we see in the people in those studies. They're able to "skip it." You can't do that when you're young; you don't dare skip it because you don't know what's important and what's not and you constantly think you're in danger of being toppled. Being young makes people nervous.

I remember nervous. I remember being nervous about everything from pleasing my parents to going to cocktail parties—the old will-anyone-talk-to-me jitters; I remember being nervous—even occasionally apoplectic—about dates, especially when I liked him more than he liked me, which seemed always to be the case, even when it was not. I remember being convinced I couldn't do the job, whatever it was. I remember sitting at the ballet, which I have always loved, and losing control of my thoughts as they wandered to a writing or TV assignment that I feared wouldn't work out—even though it usually did. Nervousness, fear, and worry can be useful, but it's blissful to be free—or freer—from all of that.

Life is no longer about the kill. It's no longer about getting: getting somewhere, getting out from under the competition, getting kudos from the boss, getting rich, getting even, getting. All that is over. Does that sound depressing? It's not. It might be, if *not* getting were all there was to it, but now it's simply getting something else: different work, maybe, that you like doing; people whom you like being with; peace, tranquillity (golf? I suppose so).

Of course, there are elderly people who feel as if they get nothing. There is such a thing as geriatric depression. Depression is the exception, not the rule, however. Researchers have found that depression symptoms are highest in young adulthood and decrease thereafter. In a national study, "major depressive episodes" were highest among twenty-five- to forty-four-year-olds and lowest among those over sixty-five. And in one of his studies, George Vaillant, the Harvard psychiatrist who, for many years, has been looking into the way people age, tells us that, as they age, people cope better with life. They show an increase in what he calls "allocentric thinking," which means the opposite of egocentric, which in a nutshell means less me, me, me. In addition, his studies show that, in dealing with setbacks, the elderly tend to use detachment and humor.

So, folks, listen up: Stay physically healthy and the bright side of aging is yours! Having left my own youth behind, I can report on the onset of aging firsthand: awesome.

# Recurrence

Okay, you've had your bum rap. You've survived and then some. And that's it. Except sometimes that's not it. Sometimes there's another blow that you hadn't seen coming (does one ever sees them coming?) behind the first. Your new husband or wife turns out to be a reptile; three months after you've rebuilt your house, there's another tornado; your cancer recurs. Seismic shocks, these repeat blows. Because even though you knew something like this *could* happen, you thought it wouldn't. Then it does. And life does another flip.

My second cancer was in a lymph node on the same side as my first mastectomy, found when my surgeon shoved his thumb in my armpit during a routine checkup. In a minute I went from happy face—somehow, I never panicked before checkups—to full-blown fear face. It was a Friday (why is it always a Friday?), and I wouldn't know the results of the biopsies until the following week. On Saturday my husband, Ed, and I flew to Milwaukee, where I was supposed to add my wisdom (ha!) on some kind of a breast-cancer panel. Funny thing is, I was probably never in better form. Being in escape mode can do that. It makes you concentrate fiercely on anything that is not the thing you're trying to escape. I felt good about my performance. I felt good about my cheery countenance. (The power thing had kicked in: See how I'm toughing this out!)

On Tuesday I learned the good news and the bad news. The neck was clear. The node under my arm was malignant. Seemed it had just been hanging around there for eight years after the mastectomy, waiting to be discovered. It was removed, of course, and radiation followed every day for five weeks. Radiation doesn't hurt. You lie there under a huge machine and a friendly technician puts your body in place, runs out of the room, zaps you with whatever they zap you with, and that's it. For me the hard part was the waiting room, which was filled with people with gray faces, some in wheelchairs. After eight years I was back in cancerland. It got me down.

When the five weeks were over, I slept a lot and woke up and felt fine. Here (again!) like a sudden blast of light, the bright side made its appearance: The sky was blue, the sun shone, the streets in New York were full of people, and I was one of them! Walking purposefully to work and then to Bloomingdale's! Life! Life had returned! Hadn't I expected it to? Not exactly. Because when you're sick—

even if you're not all *that* sick—no matter what your head tells you, you feel you'll never be well. Imagine the thrill. Never mind. You can't unless you've been there.

Same for many people after a second divorce. We all seem wired to go on, however many times we get shot down. And just as there has been a repeat of the bad stuff, there is often a repeat of the good stuff. There are some enviable third marriages. Or live ins. Or trips to Brazil.

Still, one's good sportsmanship can be tested.

November 1984: My husband, Ed, was giving a talk in Australia, and I was about to join him. He had taught in Australia before we married, had special feelings about the place, and wanted me to see it. In October I had had the yearly mammogram of my one breast and was told all was well. Early in November, a week or so before I was to leave, I gave a talk in New Orleans—by now I had begun giving cheery cancer talks—and since this one was in a hospital, I was asked if I would like a tour. That sounded pretty boring, but I wanted to be nice. So I said sure, and off we went.

I remember my guides because they were so unusual—dark-haired, female, pretty, identical-twin radiologists. They paused in front of a darkened room with an odd-looking machine, which they said was a light scanner. "Never heard of a light scanner," I said. "Want to try it?" they said, meaning on my remaining breast. "Sure," I said again, still aiming to please. I planted myself in front of the machine, and my breast was projected on a screen. What I remember next was an odd, weighty silence. Although the room was dark, I saw that the radiologists' identical faces had identical expressions. The expressions were shock.

Fortunately, I had already given my cheery cancer talk.

I called my surgeon when I got to the airport. "Piece of junk," he said when I told him about the light scanner. "But come into the office tomorrow and we'll have a look at you."

I never made it to Australia. Instead, a day after the mastectomy, Ed got on a plane, flew all night and part of the next day back to New York, and stumbled into my hospital room looking worse than I did. One of the penalties of love, as everyone knows, is that the awful thing that has happened to one happens to the other as well. Looking at my husband, unshaven, deep circles under his eyes, I thought, He did not need this.

Cancer the second—or third—time is different from the first. (Same, I think, with heart attacks.) Mainly, it's scarier. As an experienced cancer girl, I knew that this could be another round of disease, that it might have invaded other parts of my body, my bones, say, which could mean Curtains.

I felt sorrier for myself this time, and I felt angry, too.

I'm not the sort who speaks to God, but if I were, I would have said, "Hey, what gives? I have already been there and done this! Enough already! And what about poor Ed? What's he done to deserve this?"

Then I learned the cancer hadn't spread and every bit of anger evaporated and, instead, I melted into a puddle of glee. Glee, in fact, made me weepy. "I'm so lucky!" I wailed. Plus, I felt quite well. Breast cancer doesn't usually hurt, remember, and an amputation in no way compares with the removal of an internal part, such as, say, a stomach or a spleen. The night of surgery I ate dinner, for heaven's sake. And there were those recovery muscles, still pumped up from the last go-around. I knew I could handle this because I'd handled it before. That simple.

So there's recurrence and there's recurrence. If you get the kind that recurs with a spread, that is sobering. Yet I have met people with metastasized cancers who, emotionally, seem remarkably okay. They converse, they smile. For some, I suppose, the smile is a mask. For others, it's clearly what they're feeling. Against all reason, they, too, have found a bright side. Some of them are serene, others are feisty nose-thumbers. They *will* not be undone by this. They *will* live as long and as well as they possibly can. As much as I resist the word *inspiring*, it must be used here. These people own it.

# *Gratitude*

. . . . . . . . . . . . . . . . . . . . . . . . . . . . . . . . . . . . . . . . . . . . . . . . . . . . . . . . . . . . . . . .

I t seems to me, of all the bright sides to life's disasters, gratitude is the brightest, the one that emits the purest pleasure. To feel grateful if you're religious is to feel blessed. To feel grateful if you're not religious is to feel lucky. Either way, it's the sort of feeling that, at its height, makes you practically hurt with joy. Gratitude is life's best present, no doubt about it.

Nobody feels grateful all the time. That's not how it works. But if gratitude is part of your makeup—especially, I think, if it's been acquired through pain—it continually surfaces, sometimes in the oddest ways.

We have a potted hydrangea on our terrace that was clearly about to expire. There's nothing so special about a hydrangea—this one didn't even have those giant flowers some of them have; its flowers were just average. I am not a gardener, but I did my best to save it, and it got saved. And each spring when it blooms, I feel ridiculously moved, grateful for its life. As I am for my own.

Nobody can define happiness, but when you're feeling

grateful, you know you're in the neighborhood. Try feeling gloomy and grateful all at once. You can't. There's no way to do that. Gratitude picks you up and puts you in a place where gloom cannot thrive.

Happiness, I think, is a self-conscious thing. Some people might have it—with or without having had a spell of overwhelming darkness in their lives—but they often don't know it. So in a way they don't have it. Those of us who have lived through a spell of darkness have it and know it. Occasionally, we are bores about it. I like to cook. So do a lot of people. But when I turn out a carrot soup that is creamy without cream, that even my husband—not a flatterer by nature—pronounces delicious, I morph into one of those housewives in a sixties TV commercial gazing at her shiny floors with a big, stupid smile on her face.

Gratitude trumps other stuff, such as anger, sorrow, fear, even impatience. Try getting furious at the plumber who's an hour late while you're feeling grateful for your life. Maybe you feel furious, but not *as* furious, or even if you are as furious, the fury runs out of steam. You talk to yourself a lot more now, and when you do, you say things like "The plumber's late, but it's not cancer." That becomes a sort of mantra: "It's the worst haircut I've ever had in my life, but it's not cancer. . . . I missed my flight, but it's not cancer. . . . I completely overcooked the lamb, but it's not cancer. . . . I'm having a root canal tomorrow morning, but it's not. . . ."

Some combination of age and back-burner fear has gradually shrunk my ambition. That's a happy thing, believe me. All my life I have been what used to be called "a career girl." That means I not only worked like an animal but I also worked at moving up, all the time up, up. Up is over for me. I still work, I still love to work, but I'm not on a ladder. In the back of my mind I think, I still think, I could get sick again, and this time maybe I won't recover like the other times, and what matters? Altitude? I don't think so.

You don't get happiness off the rack. It's strictly made-to-order. Carrot soup won't do it for many people. I know that. It wouldn't do it for me if there weren't a bunch of other things on the table. And of course, some of those other things are not things. They're noticing how sweet the air smells after a soaking rain, or locking eyes with a four-month-old, or finding a perfect birthday present for someone I care about. It's coming home. It's putting the key in the lock and feeling the cylinder turn and knowing it's the right key in the right door. I do that every day, and as I do, I can't help noticing that (1) I am still breathing, and (2) I'm really happy about that. Grateful, too; grateful from the top of my head to my toes.

Gratitude

I confess I do not feel grateful to God. I long ago abandoned the idea that there is a Being up there somewhere who decides that one person should suffer and die and another should live. If that is the case, why me, why have I been among those who have lived? I'm not in any way nicer, better, or more valuable than people who suffer and die. I don't have children or siblings or parents, so no one would miss me that much, except my husband, and I expect he'd recover, as most spouses eventually do, I think, especially the men.

Who lives or who dies (I suppose two-pack-a-day cigarette smokers and victims of genetic flaws are exceptions) makes no sense. This is hard to swallow for a lot of people who, especially if they survive, like to think that God especially favors them. Others, who need to find logic where none exists, can find it among an array of con artists who dish out bogus explanations for diseases of all kinds—and offer "cures"—for a fee. My favorite—not!—is a woman on the West Coast who will tell you in her array of pricey packaged materials (books, cards, audiocassettes, audio CDs, videos, newsletters, lectures, calendars, and kits) that this kind of cancer is caused by being too passive, that kind of cancer comes from being too high-strung.

Having—angrily—rejected that sort of thing, I am still wildly grateful for having survived, but I feel somewhat sad, sometimes, about having no one to be grateful to. Not a day goes by that I don't want to say thank you, but to whom? My surgeon, in part, but only in part, because no matter how wonderful the surgeon, he or she can do only so much.

I envy those who have someone to thank. I read a short account in *The New York Times Magazine* once of a man in New Jersey who had served in the army in World War II and escaped from a Fascist prison camp in Italy. Sick, starving, and filthy, he was taken in by a young farm couple who would have been shot if they had been caught helping him. They fed him "sausages and steaming polenta," and gave him a real bed with clean sheets to sleep in. After the war, the soldier found the couple, and when he learned they longed to go to America, he promptly brought them to his hometown in New Jersey, where they are still living. The soldier has since died, at the age of ninety-three. One hears about people dying with "unfinished business." I don't know about the rest of his life, but this man, as he took his last breath, must have had some sense of completion.

Meanwhile, we who have had bum raps and have the riches of life still available to us have no one to bring to New Jersey. Unless we buy the God-loves-me-in-particular concept, we must be content to spend the rest of our lives feeling grateful, humbly grateful, period.

Some of my friends get depressed when their birthdays, especially the zero ones, come around. Not too long ago, I hit a big zero birthday. I rejoiced. (As in, Goody, I'm getting old!) This is not a popular stance. And when I talk about my birthday—which I do—I incur the wrath of some school and college mates, who point out that, by revealing my age, I reveal theirs. It's not that I'm crazy about the downward pull of gravity on my face, the occasional ache in my lower back, or that I have fallen into the somewhat embarrassing habit of an afternoon nap. But I feel so deeply thrilled to be old because being old means being here. I read obituaries of women who are fifty-six when they die. Why them? Why not me? No reason, no reason at all.

Post–bum raps, I am happy. Just because I can't tell you exactly what that means doesn't mean I don't feel it. I feel it, and I am determined to continue to feel it. You may think that you can't legislate happiness in this way, that you are or you aren't happy. And it isn't as if I still don't do gloom. I do it every morning jointly with my husband when I read the front page of the newspaper or when little bad things happen to me and to others. Still, I squeeze as much happiness— what feels like happiness to me—out of life as I can, and that turns out to be rather a lot. I now know, as I didn't before life nearly skidded to a halt, that, no matter what, there is usually a bright side up for grabs. One needs only to grab it.

# Notes

INTRODUCTION

xiii *"psychological immune system"*:    Daniel Gilbert, *Stumbling on Happiness* (New York: Alfred A. Knopf, 2006).

xiv *UCLA study of breast-cancer survivors:*    Annette L. Stanton, Patricia A. Ganz, Lorna Kwan, Beth E. Meyerowitz, Julienne E. Bower, Janice L. Krupnick, Julia H. Rowland, Beth Leedham, and Thomas R. Belin, "Outcomes from the Moving Beyond Cancer Psychoeducational, Randomized, Controlled Trial with Breast Cancer Patients," *Journal of Clinical Oncology,* vol. 22, no. 25 (September 1, 2005), pp. 6,009–18.

xv *studies of AIDS patients:*    Susan Folkman, "Positive Psychological States and Coping with Severe Stress," *Social Science and Medicine,* vol. 45, no. 8 (1997), pp. 1,207–21.

DOCTORS

30 *Studies of autopsies show that:*    Kaveh G. Shojania, M.D., Elizabeth C. Burton, M.D., Kathryn M. McDonald, M.M., and Lee Goldman, M.D. M.P.H., "Changes in Rates of Autopsy-Detected Diagnostic Errors over Time," *Journal of the American Medical Association,* vol. 289, no. 21 (June 4, 2003).

THE STUDIES

35 *"post-traumatic growth"*:    Richard G. Tedeschi and Lawrence G. Calhoun, "The Posttraumatic Growth Inventory: Measuring the Positive Legacy of Trauma," *Journal of Traumatic Stress,* vol. 9, no. 3 (July 1996), pp. 455–72.

36 *"learning about one's strength"*:    Christopher G. Davis, Susan Nolen-Hoeksema, and Judith Larson, "Making Sense of Loss and

Benefiting from the Experience: Two Construals of Meaning," *Journal of Personality and Social Psychology*, vol. 75, no. 2 (August 1998), pp. 561–74.

37   *115 refugees after the earthquakes of El Salvador:*   Carmelo Vázquez, Priscilla Cervellón, and Pau Pérez-Sales, "Positive Emotions in Earthquake Survivors in El Salvador (2001),"*Journal of Anxiety Disorders*, vol. 19, no. 3 (2005), pp. 313–28.

38   *1,198 Vietnam veterans were interviewed:*   Alan Fontana and Robert Rosenheck, "Psychological Benefits and Liabilities of Traumatic Exposure in the War Zone," *Journal of Traumatic Stress*, vol. 11, no. 3 (July 1998), pp. 485–503.

38   *People with Rheumatoid arthritis were asked:*   Sharon Danoff-Burg and Tracey A. Revenson, "Benefit-Finding Among Patients with Rheumatoid Arthritis: Positive Effects on Interpersonal Relationships," *Journal of Behavioral Medicine*, vol. 28, no. 1 (February 2005), pp. 91–103.

39   *At both 7 weeks and 8 years:*   Glenn Affleck, Howard Tennen, and Sydney Croog, "Causal Attribution, Perceived Benefits, and Morbidity After a Heart Attack: An 8-Year Study," *Journal of Consulting and Clinical Psychology*, vol. 55, no. 1 (February 1987), pp. 29–35.

39   *After a tornado hit Madison, Florida:*   J. Curtis McMillen, Elizabeth M. Smith, and Rachel H. Fisher, "Perceived Benefit and Mental Health After Three Types of Disaster," *Journal of Consulting and Clinical Psychology*, vol. 65, no. 5 (October 1997), pp. 733–39.

40   *In a study comparing how younger and older people:*   Susan Folkman, Richard S. Lazarus, Scott Pimley, and J. Novacek, "Age Differences in Stress and Coping Processes," *Psychology and Aging*, vol. 2, no. 2 (June 1987), pp. 171–84.

40   *Caregiving partners of men with AIDS:*   Susan Folkman, Judy T. Moskowitz, E. Ozer, and Crystal L. Park, *Coping with Chronic Stress* (New York: Plenum Press, 1997).

## MEN

63 *"Our hearts almost touched"* and *"We were always taking our pulse":* Marc Silver, *Breast Cancer Husband* (New York: Rodale Books, 2004).

## MOMENTS

68 *"moments are savored":* Laura L. Carstensen et al., "Emotional Experience in Everyday Life Across the Adult Life Span," *Journal of Personal Social Psychology,* vol. 79 (2000), pp. 644–55.

## AGING

89 *In a large study (of four communities . . . ):* J. J. Gross et al., "Emotion and Aging: Experience, Expression, and Control," *Psychology and Aging,* vol. 12 (1997), pp. 590–99.

89 *Another study . . . shows that older people:* Laura L. Carstensen et al., "Emotional Experience in Everyday Life Across the Adult Life Span," *Journal of Personal Social Psychology,* vol. 79 (2000), pp. 644–55.

91 *Whereas in yet another study adults reported:* Kira S. Birditt, Karen L. Fingerman, and David M. Almeida, "Age Differences in Exposure and Reactions to Interpersonal Tensions: A Daily Diary Study," *Psychology and Aging,* vol. 20, no. 2 (June 2005), pp. 330–40.

91 *And among 32,029 Americans ages eighteen to eighty-nine:* "The Effect of Age on Positive and Negative Affect: A Developmental Perspective on Happiness," Daniel K. Mroczek, Christian M. Kolarz, *Journal of Personality and Social Psychology,* vol. 75, no. 5 (November 1998), pp. 1,333–49.

94 *"major depressive episodes" were highest among:* Jerome K. Myers, "Six-Month Prevalence of Psychiatric Disorder in Three Communities: 1980 to 1982," *Archives of General Psychiatry,* vol. 41, no. 10 (October 1984), pp. 959–67.

94 *And in one of his studies, George Vaillant:* George E. Vaillant, *Adaptation to Life* (Boston: Little, Brown, 1977).

## About the Author

BETTY ROLLIN is a writer and an award-winning TV journalist. A former correspondent for NBC News, she now contributes reports for PBS's *Religion & Ethics Newsweekly*. Once a writer and editor for both *Vogue* and *Look* magazines, she has written for many national publications, including *The New York Times*. She is the best-selling author of six previous books, including *First, You Cry* and *Last Wish*. She lives in New York City with her husband, a mathematician.